Shots of Awesome

By

Anshu Patre

Copyright © 2022 Anshu Patre

All rights reserved....

ISBN: 9798847945257

1
Self-Determination

Goals + Drive = Mastery

Self determination is the ability to control the course of your life by conscious choice. It involves harmonizing your inner intentions with external results. It is all about personal power. Let's quickly ask: What is power? It is the ability to produce an intended effect in the world. It is your ability to desire something, act on that desire, and then achieve the intended result.

When you are powerless, the external world pushes you around without your consent. It is chaos as variables beyond your control push you down life paths that are unforeseen and unknown. Science has shown when a person feels powerless, they are much less likely to be healthy, happy, and effective. Whether you have an internal locus of control or whether that control is external to you is what determines your level of self-determination.

How does one lose the capacity for self-determination? That's easy. Just don't have any goals. Without goals, you are a raft without a paddle in the river of life. The currents will take you wherever they want. Also, if you want to lose your personal power, allow external conditions to dictate your internal state. Do drugs. Give in to peer pressure. Allow the economic and cultural conditions of your society to tell you how to act, think, and feel.

In order to be self-determined, you need goals, drive, and mastery. First, you cannot determine your life unless you know what you want out of life. Goals are essential for that reason. The world will push you around until you have a vision and a target. The second factor, drive, is necessary once you have that vision. Drive is the gas in your engine. It provides the energy you need in order to overcome the obstacles and challenges that stand between you and your goal.

Drive involves the act of motivation, and there are two sources of motivation: extrinsic and intrinsic. You can push yourself because of external things such as money. Or you can push yourself because you have passion, purpose, and a desire for mastery. Competence and skill are the inevitable result of having goals and drive. You need the ability to handle the challenges of life, and those challenges can only be overcome by mastery.

So what is mastery? I define it as one's ability to confront the chaos of the world and bring order out of that chaos. It is your ability to respond to life's demands as they come up. Mastery is when you have put so much time and practice into your personal growth and habits that you are capable of actualizing your highest life potential. Many people are good at their craft, but they do not become the best because they fail to perform the process routines that support their best work. If you want to be a good writer, you don't just have to write a lot. You have to eat healthy, exercise, work hard, meditate, and many other things in order to get your brain firing and wiring in the right direction. Mastery is holistic. If you want to be the best, do not simply focus on one thing. Instead focus on the process of improving everything.

> "Mastery is not a function of genius or talent.
> It is a function of time and intense effort
> applied to a particular field of knowledge."
> Robert Greene

2
Happiness

Purpose + Plan = The Good Life

So first and foremost: What is happiness? I define it in relation to two psychological constructs. First, there is the *experiencing self*, your actual feelings. Happiness requires that you feel joy, love, and serenity regularly. It is the frequency of positive vs. negative emotions. Second, there is the *thinking self*, which is the story-making machine in your head. Happiness also relates to the meaning and significance that you consciously or unconsciously attach to your life and the universe in general. Happiness requires growth, the belief that your life matters, that it is going somewhere.

Now, how do we live richer and more fulfilling lives? By understanding the essential nature of each self. The experiencing self is an entity that exists in contradiction to the thinking self. When thinking stops, experiencing begins. One way to live happily is to live in the moment, allowing the experiencing self to emerge by listening to music. When you take the time to simply breathe and notice, once you stop fretting about the past or imagining the future, then the experiencing self is able to feel peace and joy consistently.

Yet thinking is essential to the makeup of our minds. It is easy to tell people to stop thinking. It is much harder to actually do it. Therefore, you must train your thinking mind by using optimism, which means looking forward to a bright future. This is one way to effectively imprint the thinking mind with positivity. The second way, which is tied to optimism, involves finding deeper meaning and purpose in your life. When you have direction, when you know what your life is about, then happiness becomes your constant companion because no action is taken without awareness of larger goals. The rest of this book revolves around these two projects. Finding happiness and finding purpose in life. Here is a thought exercise that elicits both purpose and optimism.

(1) Imagine yourself three years in the future. Imagine everything that you want and desire coming to you. Imagine your goals coming true.

(2) Now, make those dreams your purpose in life, and then make a plan to achieve that purpose.

This means you have to imagine what you want in detail. Then make a specific, measurable, realistic, time-constrained plan for getting there. Simple two step process: Set a goal. Make a plan to achieve it.

3
Myths of Happiness

$$Happiness = \frac{Reality}{Expectation}$$

The book, the Myths of Happiness, has just shown me how unconscious people really are. And it's not their fault. Our self-obsessed culture brainwashes them, creating a putrid lens that distorts our vision of reality. Written by a psychologist current with the latest findings in the field of happiness, Sonja Lyubomirsky, it turns out that most humans are woefully ignorant about what makes them happy. Here is what DOES NOT make you happy (but you think it does)

1. Having an Easy and Perfect Life.
Research shows that those who experience adversity end up happier and more grateful for their blessings.

2. Passionate Marriages
While they do boost happiness for two years, positive emotions eventually return to earlier set points.

3. Reaching a Goal
Positive emotions derived from goal attainment are fleeting, lasting at most a week or two.

4. Money (after a point)

Money spent on things does not make us happy. Money spent on novel experiences does.

5. Being Highly Educated

One study found that the more educated you are, the less satisfied you are with your life.

6. Materialism

Dozens of studies prove that materialistic people are less happy, have weaker relationships, share less with others, pollute the environment, etc.

7. Intense Moments of Bliss

While these experiences are wonderful, happy people are those who experience a steady stream of positive feeling and emotion. This implies that fancy vacations do not make the woman happy. Small habits that skip material stimuli and go straight to the brain do the job.

Here is what DOES make you happy (but you just don't care)

1. Being Grateful

Hedonic adaptation, the process of getting used to external conditions, is less likely to occur if you consistently express gratitude. Studies in which participants express gratitude once a week for ten weeks, or pen appreciation letters to their loved ones, result in greater health and happiness up to six months later.

2. Helping Others

Studies show that spending time and money on others boosts happiness more than spending it on oneself.

3. Physical Touch

Touch activates the reward pathways of our brains. It boosts positive mood and reduces stress.

4. New and Varied Experiences

Our dopamine pathways get used to repetitive stimuli. They fire bright when new things come along.

5. Striving towards Meaningful Goals

Constant little bursts of pleasure come from progressing towards our goals. We deal with the existential hole in our souls by filling it with meaningful and selfless pursuits.

6. Meditation

Meditation lights up neurons related to empathy and positive emotion. It bolsters the immune system and alleviates stress. It increases intelligence and focus power.

7. Nature

Nature rests and rejuvenates the mind. Experiments comparing a walk in nature to a busy street show that the former leads to better focus and engagement. And nature boosts happiness too.

8. Deep Relationships

Compared to dozens of other factors, it turns out that love, the meaningful connection, is easily the most powerful determinant of our happiness.

9. Spirituality

Studies show that spiritual people tend to be happier than materialists.

Countless studies have affirmed and re-affirmed the findings discussed above. But if this is true, then why are we so confused all the time? Well, I think two thoughts give us one strong reason. First, it has to do with the unconscious. We now know that most of our drives arise from areas inaccessible to the conscious mind. Some scientists say that we only experience about 5% of the operations carried out by the brain, while the rest is totally beyond our reach. Connect this idea to the fact that we underestimate the power of social scripts and culture on our belief structures, and you have a good reason as to why people are so amazingly vapid.

Social scripts provide us with "culturally acceptable" (but incorrect) reasons for our unconscious impulses. When American culture tells you to make money, buy trinkets, get a PhD, get a "respectable" job, avoid struggle, and all of these other things, you are being forced to follow social scripts created by the unconscious people around you.

But the beginning of self-awareness comes from knowing our own unconscious biases. Here's a thought experiment to illustrate your own. I'll show you a list of words. I want you to (out loud) say hello for happy adjectives and the things that cause happiness (according to our culture), and I want you to say good-bye for sad adjectives and the things that cause sadness (according to our culture).

Happy, Sad, island vacation, 60 hr work week, Depressed, poverty, Joy, failing to become a doctor, Peace!, Love!, shopping spree, going homeless, becoming a doctor, Bliss, Anger, losing your mother, winning the lottery, Delighted, Gloomy.

Well, I'm sure that was easy. Now, I want you to (out loud) say hello for happy adjectives and the things that cause sadness, and say goodbye for the sad adjectives and the things that cause happiness.

Happy, Sad, island vacation, 60 hr work week, Depressed, poverty, Joy, failing to become a doctor, Peace!, Love!, shopping spree, going homeless, becoming a doctor, Bliss, Anger, losing your mother, winning the lottery, Delighted, Gloomy.

Tougher, right? Do you see what I mean? Our Stone-age brains and our western culture have brainwashed us into believing that material circumstances determine our happiness. Superficially, what appears as bad often, in the long run, leads to a lot of good. We just need the wisdom to see it.

"Having gone on his almsround, the sage should then go to the forest, standing or taking a seat at the foot of a tree. The enlightened one, intent on jhana, should find delight in the forest, should practice jhana at the foot of a tree, attaining his own satisfaction." The Buddha

4
Social Dimensions of Happiness

# of Good Friends x Depth of Connection = Level of Success

The scientific study of mirror neurons tells us two things: (1) These cells allow humans to simulate outer events as inner reality, effectively imprinting our neuronal pathways with the emotions felt by others. (2) Everything we are-our intelligence, personality, health, and work ethic-is partially determined by the energy and emotions of the people around us. It is all about energy at the end of the day. Is the energy around you positive or negative? New scientific research shows that 90% of the anxiety at work is caused by about 5% of the people in your social network. Meanwhile, scientists testing the biosocial dimensions of stress found that simply watching a stressed out friend can increase the amount of stress hormone, cortisol, in your own brain by 26%. Pretty depressing, right?

The good news is that happiness and enthusiasm are just as contagious. Another study analyzing the spread of happiness in social networks shows that happy people increase the probability that nearby friends are happy by 63%. Women with good systems of social support live 2.8 years longer (2.3 years for men) on average than women without deep connections to friends and family. And consider all of the health benefits of good company: (1) It inoculates us against cognitive decline and dementia, (2) it improves immune function, and (3) it even reduces the intensity of pain if you happen to be sick.

Humans are genetically tailored to bond in tight social groups, so it comes as no surprise that our relationships have the greatest impact on sustained happiness when compared to money or social status. Bottom line: You should only spend time with three types of people: those that make you happy, those that make you better, and those that make you money. So now that we know about the power of social connections, let's talk about the simple steps needed to maximize happiness and minimize stress.

1. Write down and prioritize your goals.

2. Look at your inner social circle; the ten or so people that you communicate the most with.

3. Ask yourself who drains your energy, models negative behaviors, and takes you further from your goals. Eliminate interactions with them.

4. Now that you have some space in your inner circle, make it a point to bond with positive people; people who are going to push you to be your best self.

Happiness and Health

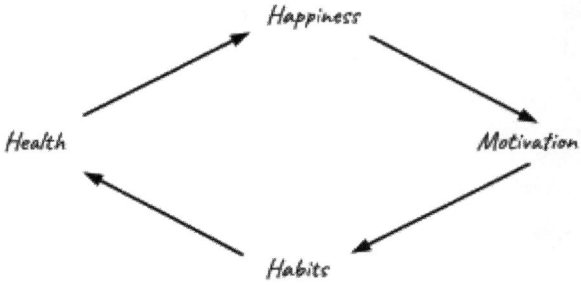

One telling study on happiness and health involved the autobiographies of 180 Catholic nuns. Near the age of 22, they were asked to briefly recount their lives. Their short writings were then rated on a happiness meter depending on the words they used. Here are two examples.

Sister 1 (low positive emotion): I was born on September 26, 1909, the eldest of seven children, five girls and two boys...My candidate year was spent in the Motherhouse, teaching Chemistry and Second Year Latin at Notre Dame Institute. With God's grace, I intend to do my best for our Order, for the spread of religion and for my personal sanctification.

Sister 2 (high positive emotion): God started my life off well by bestowing upon me a grace of inestimable value.... The past year which I have spent as a candidate studying at Notre Dame College has been a very happy one. Now I look forward with eager joy to receiving the Holy Habit of Our Lady and to a life of union with Love Divine.

The rating scale was incredibly rigorous, and when six decades had passed, the data showed strong connections between happiness and longevity. On average, the happiest nuns lived nearly a decade longer than the unhappiest. The wonderful thing about nuns is that they all live very similar lives, so any difference in lifespan would likely come from inner qualities as opposed to external conditions.

From such studies, the field of psychoneuroimmunology was born. Researchers from Harvard to Stanford have found that human emotions affect the autonomic nervous system, and that this system goes on to alter immune function. There are three major toxic emotions: anger, anxiety, and depression. Hundreds of studies show chronic negative emotions can double the risk of heart disease, cancer, and general sickness. Why does this happen? When the body feels extreme negativity, it imagines that your very survival is being threatened, and so it diverts energy away from normal functioning to deal with the imagined threat.

For example, one Yale study followed 929 survivors of heart attack. It found that those prone to anger were three times more likely to die of cardiac arrest than calmer patients. Another study of colorectal cancer patients found that those reporting high levels of stress were five times more likely to develop cancer than their stress free counterparts. And when exposed to a mild cold virus, 27% of stress free people came down with a cold compared to 47% of those living with high stress. Meanwhile, in elderly women with hip fractures, those with depression were two thirds less likely to walk again.

Pretty terrifying, right? The bright side is this: If negative emotions can do so much damage, then positive emotions can do just as much good. You can change. For those prone to anger, an emotional regulation program was able to reduce the chances of having a second heart attack by 44%. Another study surveyed 122 sick men for levels of optimism and pessimism. Of the 25 most pessimistic, 21 had died eight years later. Of the 25 most optimistic, only 6 had died. There is one obvious reason for such findings. Happy people take better care of their bodies. The less clear reason is that positive emotions directly boost biological function. There is some evidence that happiness benefits the cardio-vascular and immune systems, and it is undeniable that it influences hormones and inflammation levels. So, what does science tell us? The same thing that the ancients knew for eons.

> "A good laugh and a long sleep
> are the two best cures for anything."
> ~ Irish Proverb

6
Dynamics of Pleasure

Current Pleasure x Future Meaning = Level of Happiness

All humans are born with certain innate drives. We all desire food and sleep. We desire mates and children. And most universal of all is our attraction to pleasure and avoidance of pain. Why do we pursue pleasure? Many say that it is an end in itself. They say that happiness is pleasure, and that there is no distinction between the two. But I think they are wrong. Pleasure is not happiness. Just look at your own experience. When you gorge yourself on ice cream, the fifth scoop never tastes as good as the first, which brings us to our first quality of pleasure. Pleasure follows the law of diminishing returns. The more you get of it, the less valuable it becomes.

Pleasure also comes from external sources. Some outer activity is always required to attain it. Whether you want sex, food, or nice vacations, pleasure arises from the stimulation of the body, and anything based on the body means that the sensations are fleeting. And things that are fleeting can never give you the deeper happiness that comes from finding purpose in life. Pleasure focuses on the self without consideration for others. Meanwhile, happiness requires the holistic view; a total view of one's life and whether it is fulfilling its deeper ambitions, dreams, and desires.

We humans have another deep drive within us. It is the drive to create. While pleasure is based on consumption, there is something inside of us that wants to produce and create. We want to give something of ourselves to the world. This deeper meaning is why happiness is so different from pleasure. When you have meaning in your life, even pain and setbacks add fuel to the fire. Meaning creates sustainable and consistent happiness. Meaning comes from somewhere beyond the body, so it isn't fleeting or transient. And finally, meaning provides direction in your life, which leads to growth, and growth is one of the biggest contributors to happiness.

> "Enjoy present pleasures in such a way
> so as not to injure future ones."
> - Seneca

7

The Meaningful Life

Imagine a funeral. But this is not just anyone's funeral. It's your funeral. Perhaps, your body lies in a fancy casket, or your family gathers to spread your ashes across the Ganges. Before the final goodbye, your child gets up in front of the group and says...what? That you created life and love for those around you; that your presence on this earth was a positive ripple that will be felt for generations? Or will they mumble a few platitudes because you actually spent the fleeting moments of life chasing meaningless pleasures?

Go deeply into this vision. Close your eyes and use your imagination. When I did the exercise, I understandably felt sad, but there was also a new drive to make the most of my life and improve the lives of those around me. When you go, nobody will remember your nice car or fancy vacations. They will remember how you made them feel...for good or for ill. Bronnie Ware, an Australian nurse who has spent years with people in the last months of their lives, found that there are five common regrets that people have when the end finally comes.

> 1. I wish I'd had the courage to live a life true to myself, not the life others expected of me.

2. I wish I hadn't worked so hard.

3. I wish I had the courage to express my feelings.

4. I wish I had stayed in touch with my friends.

5. I wish I had let myself be happier.

In consequence, I can come up with five remedies that you need to apply right now to your life.

1. Never Settle for Mediocrity.
2. Enjoy Your Work or Work Less
3. Be You. Do You. For You.
4. Stay in Touch with Your Friends
5. Happiness is Under Your Control

Right now, there is the actual you and there is the potential you. What you are versus what you can become. To actualize your highest potential is the only way to real, lasting happiness, whether it is being an amazing mother, doctor, or artist. For Aristotle eudaimonia requires arete. That is, human flourishing and happiness depend on excellence and mastery of one's purpose in life. Abraham Maslow saw self-actualization as a fundamental need in human nature. Once biological and social needs are met, optimal living becomes as essential as the air we breathe. So go out and paint that painting, read that book on enlightened parenting, volunteer for something, or just go spend some quality time with your kids.

These are the things that people miss the most when the end finally comes. Think I'm kidding? Ask the mountaineers trapped in a blizzard on Mt. Everest. When faced with the certainty of death, they weren't thinking about missing that episode of Keeping Up with the Kardashians. They were thinking about their loved ones, their untapped potential, and how much time they wasted when the going was good. Meaning. Purpose. Human Flourishing. This is what truly matters in life, and we realize this, almost paradoxically, by contemplating our own inevitable demise. Contemplating death is undeniably a sad thing. But it's incredibly generative in the long run. It's like using manure as fertilizer...fertilizer for the garden of life.

At the end of the day, happiness requires meaning and meaning, at least minimally, requires a dose of altruistic morality. Being happy almost necessitates that one finds purpose in life and in what they do. Studies find that, no matter their occupation, some people see their work as a calling because they care about others, while others see their work as a chore because they just want money. Scientists have interviewed happy janitors who feel their work really matters, and unhappy doctors that just want to make it through the day.

Maximizing Potential

Time + Talent = Skill

Skill + Opportunity = Success

Let's be honest. Life is suffering. It is filled with setbacks, failure, pain, and eventually death. The question is: How can we go beyond this suffering? What can we give ourselves, psychologically, to master life on life's terms? The answer's simple. We can maximize our potential and self actualize at some craft. But this requires three internal resources and two external resources. In terms of inner resources, self actualization requires talent, hard work, and focus. (1) We have to be good at it. (2) We have to work to get better at it. And (3) we cannot divert our attention away from it. That is, we can't wander down too many avenues, and must instead stick to one overarching life goal.

When we do this, we are more likely to self actualize. But it isn't guaranteed. We need two external structures to maximize our talent: time and opportunity. (1) We need to be given the time to maximize our potential. This means structuring your life so you can work on your craft a little everyday. And (2) thriving requires a moment; an opportunity to shine. For example, Michelangelo had his moment when he was commissioned to paint the Sistine Chapel. Gandhi self actualized due to the historical circumstances he was placed in. And finally, you can actualize by seeing and seizing your chance to display your craft. This is how you deal with the problem of suffering.

On Creativity

Idea + Implementation = Creativity

Creativity is the bread and butter of meaningful living. Bringing forth something new into the world is by far the easiest way to believe that your life is worth living; that it is going somewhere. But what exactly is creativity, and how do we program it into our lives? That is the topic of this section.

First, let's find a working definition of creativity. Creativity is the process of both generating a novel idea in thought, and then implementing that idea in reality. So how does one generate a novel idea? It requires two phases: (1) the gathering and memorization of information and (2) the process of integrating that information into your unconscious mind.

First, you have to focus on a problem for a long time. You need expertise in the area that you want to innovate within. For example, Einstein needed to know mathematics and physics in order to construct his theory of general relativity. Second, after intensely focusing on a problem or idea, you let it marinate in your unconscious mind over many nights and weeks. You stop focusing on the problem and do something else, like go for a walk. The unconscious mind is where ideas transform and link up with other ideas. The conscious mind can only hold several bits of information at any one time. The unconscious mind is infinite in what it knows and creates.

With any luck, and by immersing yourself in some idea, your mind will have a creative insight. Perhaps, it's an idea for a new cooking recipe. Perhaps, it's an idea for a new video game. The domain of creativity is vast. But once the insight takes place, then comes the hard part. This point is why most people fail to live meaningful lives. You have to implement your creative insight no matter the struggles and setbacks that accompany any creative endeavor. Anyone can come up with an idea. But the real world makes it so only those willing to implement their ideas reap the benefits of meaningful engagement. You can't just think about writing a book. You have to sit down and write it. You can't just think your way out of any problem. You have to take creative action. Following are a few ways to stimulate creativity in your own life.

(1) Humor - Research shows that groups that laugh more are more creative in their work.
(2) Expertise - Knowing any field really well, both technically and generally, makes it more likely that you'll have a creative breakthrough.
(3) Flow - A flow state describes your immersion in a project, where time stops and you are completely in the moment.

Emotional Intelligence

In recent times, psychology has shifted from studying depressing things to studying the positive side of life, applying rigorous methods to determine what really makes humans happy. What is its most important finding? That it is possible to transform our brains into happiness generators instead of worry machines; that you have the power to create happiness within yourself.

For most of history, outer circumstances have determined our inner condition. This seems to be the result of our evolutionary past. When you live in a world where material resources matter, it is no wonder that our brains evolved to value things such as money, social status, and power. And this valuation process is largely automatic. Neuroscience tells us that there are two sets of neural activity going on in the human mind at any one time. One set happens in the lower brain, which is automatic, habitual, emotional, intuitive, subconscious, and, most importantly, involuntary and mostly out of our control. Meanwhile, the higher brain is conscious, voluntary, slow, deliberate, and, most importantly, the seat of self control capable of learning new models for behavior.

Since the emotional brain is so much older than the neocortex, it has incredible power over our thoughts and behavior. The rational mind is intricately tied to the emotional brain. Indeed, it grows out of the emotional brain like a plant. Fear, happiness, anger, sadness—each emotion takes place in different brain structures. Ideally, consciousness serves as an integrator of different neurological subroutines. Thought and emotion ought to inform each other in order to guide our behavior and decision-making processes. Meta-cognition is the ability to be aware of one's thoughts, which requires a level of detachment; a shift in the relationship between one and one's thoughts. Meta-emotion, meanwhile, involves being aware of one's emotions.

Both abilities require the top-down conscious mind, and both abilities require cultivation. The human brain is super elastic and malleable. It produces one hundred thousand neurons a day, and it turns out that many things influence this rate of production. New brain cells take about a month to mature, and another four to integrate and link up with existing brain structures. To the degree that happiness and self-control are the result of the structure, relationship, and chemical composition of the prefrontal cortex to the rest of the brain, our environment determines how good we are as humans. If you get lots of love in your life (which releases oxytocin), your brain naturally attunes to show greater compassion for others. If you take the time to write about your feelings and beliefs, your brain will naturally bend itself into a more reflective and intelligent organ. In one experiment, even if mice are genetically predisposed to having lots of oxytocin, the lack of maternal care degrades parts of the brain known to accept the molecule. We see evidence of this in humans as well. Murderous psychopaths, many of whom grow up in orphanages, are known to have difficulty inhibiting emotions and impulses, and tend to show deficits in one area of the brain in particular: the orbitofrontal cortex.

The OFC lies in between the prefrontal cortex and the midbrain-amygdala. Its job is to mediate the demands of our primal selves by using the thinking mind. It tamps down on unhealthy emotions and channels our feelings into socially appropriate responses. It is the seat of social decision making, and strengthening it is bound to result in more happiness and success down the road (especially if we start as children). So how do we strengthen the better angels of our nature to check and channel our baser impulses? Practice. Practice. Practice.

Meditation is a good way to focus the mind. Mantras light up the higher cognitive regions of the brain, while emotional intelligence strengthens the coherence of the higher and lower self. In order to weave the many parts of the brain together, we need to pump up the OFC's ability to master the amygdala by constantly asking questions like: How do I feel at this moment? Is this feeling legitimate and justified? What am I thinking right now?

The brain is so flexible that even adults lacking emotional intelligence can pick it up given enough time and practice. It's just about ingraining reflective habits into the neural pathways of your brain. Use it or lose it. That's the science of neuroplasticity. The brain is like a bridge that gets stronger the more times you drive over it. Make the right neural connections and your entire life will fall into place.

Basic Elements of Emotional Intelligence
By
Daniel Goleman

(1) Self-Awareness: Knowing One's Emotions

(2) Self-Control: Managing One's Emotions

(3) Self-Motivation: Using One's Emotions

(4) Empathy: Sensing Emotions in Others

(5) Relationships: Managing the Emotions of Other

11

Parallel Dimensions and Life Paths

"Difficult to see. Always in motion is the future." - Yoda

Imagine this. You are a being living in one tiny dimension of a much larger and deeper Reality. This Reality encompasses infinite parallel dimensions and timelines that coexist alongside each other, and inside each alternate reality resides an alternate version of yourself. Imagine yourself as a doctor. Imagine another timeline where you're a millionaire inventor. Imagine a life path that ends up in jail. Imagine marrying the girl of your dreams. Imagine dying early of drug overdose. All of these potentials exist *right now*. What makes them more than potential are our choices.

Every time you make a life altering decision, another reality and timeline branches out from the life path you're now on. Right now, there is the actual you and the potential you. Reality is a stream moving us from finite past actuality to infinite future potential. As the future turns into the past, this potential is made actual, and what transforms the infinite into finite are our choices.

Man is a self-determining creature, which means that, unlike animals and plants who must follow the course that nature sets for them, man is able to see the many paths available to him, and use this vision to determine the course of his life. And in determining this course, he determines himself; who he is, what he stands for, and how he uses his finite time on this planet. The meaning of life is to envision the highest future potential available to you, and make the choices that take you down that life path.

It's all about our choices. It's about the choices we make everyday, over and over, until the choice is no longer a choice, but a habit. The future is an infinite field of possibility. It is liquid. Every choice you make either limits or expands your choices down the road. When you choose something once, it becomes many times more likely that you'll choose it again. Good choices provide the circumstances for better choices. Bad choices lead to worse options.

Your life is a self-replicating loop. It's a system that reinforces itself. When you make a choice, you are making or unmaking yourself. But what is the self? It isn't some stable thing. Your personality, emotions, thoughts, motivations, feelings; they all change in relation to your life path, which includes your future environment, friends, job, wealth, connections, and husband/wife. Life is about the simple connection between your inner and outer reality. Wisdom is understanding how deeply these realities influence each other.

12
Conscious Mind-Sets

(...after Yoda lifts a star fighter out of this swamp using the Force on the planet, Dagobah...)
Luke Skywalker: I...I don't believe it!
Yoda: And that is why you fail...

This section is about the power of belief; about how a simple belief can limit or unleash your potential. When a belief enters your brain, it totally shapes and bends your reality. Your emotions, thoughts, actions, and life course are determined by it. The psychologist, Carol Dweck, identifies two basic belief structures that lie at the foundation of almost all our other beliefs. Either you have a fixed mindset or a growth mindset. Either you believe that human qualities are set in stone or that we all have the potential to grow and become more. If you have a fixed mindset, failure means you are a failure. If you have a growth mindset, failure means you need to work harder, get help, or try new strategies.

And these beliefs alter the trajectory of your life. In one study, college freshmen at the University of Hong Kong (a place where everything is taught in English) had the chance to take a remedial English class once it was determined that their knowledge of the language was deficient. The students were also tested to see if they had a growth or fixed mindset. Can you guess which group opted to take the remedial class and which group opted to massage their fragile egos? Yup.

And consider which mindset more accurately reflects reality. Notice the connection between mindsets and "moral character". The fixed mindset means you have to constantly struggle to validate your position in the social hierarchy, while the growth mindset actively seeks out mentors and learns from those who are older and wiser. One study followed college students who were given the chance to look at their classmates' papers after doing poorly on a test. Those with the fixed mindset looked at tests with really bad grades to make themselves feel better, while the growth mindset students looked for the top papers to see what they did wrong and how they could improve.

From this it is obvious that growth mindset kids make better grades than fixed mindset kids. And one reason is clear: When you believe that you can grow, when you know that effort creates progress towards your goals, your motivation and optimism systems totally activate. What is not so obvious is that mindsets can be implanted into people by suggestion. When two groups of students were asked to solve tough IQ questions, one group was praised for ability and the other was praised for effort. Later, they were given the choice to tackle a tougher set of problems. One simple sentence of praise created divergences between the groups. The ability-praised students refused to tackle the new problems, while 90 percent of the effort-praised kids took the initiative. As a result, the effort kids' performance went through the roof on later problems, while the ability kids' performance nosedived.

So, social context matters. The people around you influence your behavior. But the big question is: Does the mindset stick with you after you leave the lab? No. It turns out that our mindsets are deeply ingrained habits of thought. To change them requires years of focus and discipline. Neuroscience tells us that there are two sets of neural activity happening in the human brain at any one time. One set involves the lower brain; automatic, habitual, emotional, intuitive, subconscious, and, most importantly, involuntary and out of our control. Meanwhile, the higher brain is conscious, voluntary, slow, deliberate, and, most importantly, the seat of self control capable of learning new models of behavior. As a behavior becomes habitual, the higher brain passes off the routine to the lower brain. This saves energy and makes the task unconscious and automatic.

Do you ever zone out and, before you realize it, you have one hand in the pantry desperately searching for junk food? The same principle applies to mindsets. You have to lock-in with laser focus to change them. You need to meditate on the general pattern of your thoughts. Then you have to nudge those patterns away from the fixed mindset towards the optimistic growth mindset. More essentially, change the personality trait that creates the thought in the first place. Too often we go through life like zombies. But lasting change requires conscious engagement with the brain's habitual tendencies.

>Dwecks' Ideal Growth Question
>"What can I learn from this?
>What will I do next time I'm in this situation?"

13
The Danger of "Happiness"

Let me be clear. There is a massive difference between contentment and happiness, and the danger is not being able to tell them apart. Thoreau famously said that "most men live lives of quiet desperation." The most insidious thing about mediocrity is that it is bearable. It is okay. You can live with it. The question is: Should you live with it?

For two years, I worked a minimum wage job at Books A Million. I never realized how unhappy I was until a coworker pointed out my negative energy. She said, "You're a nice guy, but you always seem sad when you come in here." Boy was that news to me! I didn't believe it for months until the truth was impossible to ignore. I didn't realize it because I wasn't in tune with my energy field. My vibes were not too hot.

So the first question to ask yourself is this:
Am I truly truly happy? Am I living my life's purpose?

Asking these questions, I quickly found out that I was not on purpose. I quit my job and traveled to a monastery in California, which was a life changing experience for me. Meditating three hours a day, I really tuned into my energy and amped it up to a level of pure joy and positivity. My life changed in a matter of months. I was amazed that I could be so happy and so unaware that I was once unhappy.

The second question to ask is this:
If I am happy, then is there any way to become happier?
What radical action can I take to totally upgrade my life?

For months afterwards, I thought I had made it. I didn't really try to change my life. I just chilled. Lazy is the word for it. I thought up the idea for this book, but didn't sit down to write it. One day, I was messing around and I found my long forgotten iPod. "Hmmm?" I told myself. "Maybe, I can use this thing." That one thought totally changed my life again. It created another thought. "I should download audio-books and motivational speeches from people like Tony Robbins off youtube."

I did the math. I was in the car for about five hours a week. My car has an iPod jack, so that amounts to about 250 hours a year now devoted to self development. 250 hours!! That is a week and a half worth of hours! There are 52 weeks in a year in case you didn't know. All that time was now devoted to thoughts of self-discipline, work ethic, motivation, research for this book, and general learning.

Moral of the story: Radical action leads to massive change, and one tiny act (finding the iPod) influences the next act, and the next, and the next, in a ripple effect that quickly becomes tidal waves. No matter how content you are, ask yourself: What radical action can I take to create more purpose, happiness, and vitality in my life? Life is about growth. Grow or stagnate. It's your choice.

> "Stop wasting time in playing a role or a concept.
> Instead, learn to actualize yourself, your potential."
> ~Bruce Lee

14
Becoming World-Class Awesome

"The top level goal is not a means to any other end. It is, instead, an end in itself. I think of this top level goal as a compass that gives direction and meaning to all the goals below it." ~ Angela Duckworth

"The plain fact remains that men the world over possess vast amounts of resource, which only very exceptional individuals push to their extremes of use." ~ William James

```
                    /\
                   /  \
                  /Life\
                 /Purpose\
                /----------\
               / Life Goals \
              /--------------\
             /  Daily Habits  \
            /------------------\
           /  Structure of Time \
          /   and Doing Things   \
         /------------------------\
```

Above is a simple formula that you can use to organize your life. It gives meaning to life because it shows you how your daily tasks can be oriented towards larger aims. It helps organize your time around deeply held values and goals. Everyone's day is made up of simple moments; small tasks that take you towards your goals or away from them. The point of this exercise is to help you see whether your daily behaviors actually serve a higher purpose in life. Take a minute to write down your life goals and what daily habits you need in order to achieve them.

> "All our life, so far as it has definite form,
> is but a mass of habits."
> ~William James

So what is a habit? It is a decision that we make, stemming from interest or from coercion, which becomes an unconscious and automatic behavior over time and repetition. Duke University published a paper that said over 40 percent of our daily rituals are not conscious decisions, but unconscious bundles of neural programming wired deep into our brains. Under all of the layers of recently evolved tissue lies something called the basal ganglia, a tissue whose function was unknown until about the 1990's. Scientists at MIT discovered its function by sticking wire probes into rat brains, and then setting them loose in a maze with chocolate at the end.

Of course, at first the rats had no clue what was going on. And this is when the brain works the hardest. Their neural networks buzzed with activity as they explored their surroundings. Eventually, once they found the prize, the researchers put the same rat through the same scenario again....and again...and again...hundreds of times. As expected, the rats figured out the game and soon began to run the maze quickly and without mistakes.

Unexpectedly, neural activity quieted as the rat formed an automatic habit. The decision making centers stopped firing while the basal ganglia automatized the routine and took over. What was once a conscious exploration turned into an unconscious behavior controlled by an ancient structure near the reptilian brain stem. Amazingly, this habit storing tissue works for simple behaviors such as eating chocolate, and also complex behaviors such as writing books.

Right now, because I have made a habit out of it, my bottom up neural patterns are buzzing with the pleasure of writing. Your lower neural machinery is responsible for the activation of involuntary habits and intuitive networks of association. This may seem like it's a bad thing, but it's not. Our brain is designed to conserve energy, and this intuitive brain gets optimal results with minimal effort if we take the time to burn the habit into our neural circuits. Most people's habits emerge in their neural pathways without their deliberate choice.

But the secret is that experts do this whole thing differently. They take conscious control by understanding the structure of the habit loop in order to hack their behaviors. Habit loops are often sensitive and the slightest disturbance can knock them off course. Experts know that people change when they tinker with specific aspects of their behavioral patterns. When you feel the cue, for example the urge to smoke weed, you can replace it with another routine that yields a similar reward. Remember, our brains are not supercomputers. We have a finite amount of focusing power. Choosing positive thoughts naturally results in fewer negative thoughts. So just meditate. The practice naturally crowds out the desire for weed with the top down regulation of the prefrontal cortex.

Now when the cue to smoke weed happens, I say, "Nah, I'm good." and I sit down and meditate. Moreover, this loop can be applied to every good and bad habit of your life. Always look to optimize your routines. Make the good better and the bad non-existent. This habit formation loop underlies Angela's research in the book, Grit. Excellence in any field depends on your neural machinery being so saturated by the practice that your brain naturally optimizes those neural pathways over everything else. So what does this mean for us? It means that skill at any craft depends on doing it a lot. Experts follow routines. Talent only determines how quickly we pick up a skill, while effort goes into the equation many times over.

These are the ingredients for success at the highest level: passion, talent, and hard work. But it's not just hard work. It's a lot of hard work. Indeed, many studies show that true mastery in any field requires about 10, 000 hours of practice. That's 10 years of working at your craft for several hours a day. Now, this isn't everybody. Some people are lucky enough to have some talent. They pick up things fast. But beyond a bit of talent, once you're good enough to be among the best, it's simply about plugging away all day and all night.

In the 1990's, K. Anders Ericsson went to the Berlin Music academy and asked its professors to divide the students into three classes. Those with the potential to become world-class musicians. Those considered merely good. And those unlikely to ever become professional musicians. After this ranking process, Ericsson looked at how many hours each student had practiced across their lifespan.

> The Top Group: ~10, 000 hours
> The Middle Group: ~ 8, 000 hours
> Music Teachers: ~ 4, 000 hours

When they did this among chess players, they found that the grand champions started playing at a much younger age than the national champions. Again, Ericsson failed to find anybody that you could call a natural talent. There were no musicians that leapt into a higher group while practicing far fewer hours. On the flip side, there were no "grinds" either; those who worked harder than everyone else but failed to make it into the group they belonged to. So what does this mean? Once you have the ability to make it into the top echelon of any field of endeavor, all that matters is plugging away at it until you get to the top.

This process of shooting for a goal that you find meaningful and challenging leads to what psychologists call flow; a state of intense absorption in the moment as your bottom-up machinery naturally executes its routines without effort. You don't have to think, you just do. It's a pleasurable experience conducive to spontaneous creativity and peak performance; a reward in itself as we lose consciousness of everything except the task at hand. One precondition for this state is that the task cannot be beyond or beneath our capabilities. The other is that we need to have put in a lot of hours to train our associative and intuitive networks to fire in optimal fashion.

The experience of flow really gets you far if you have a bit of talent. But to really become an expert in any field, you also have to engage in what is called deliberate practice, a process whereby the individual takes control of the mind to consciously counteract the brain's natural impulse to automate our habits. You don't become better at things by mechanically doing the same thing over and over again. In order to get good at writing or anything else, you need to constantly question your models and systems for doing things. This means top-down, effortful, voluntary, active, and goal directed engagement with whatever you're doing. Our brains' natural impulse is to become set in its ways (which is why old people are old), while conscious self control allows us to adapt, try new habits, make contingency plans, and program emotions such as motivation and optimism into our neural pathways.

By its very definition, deliberate practice is not fun. It can only be engaged in when the challenge is tougher than our skill set. It involves breaking our craft into processes and several components, observing other peoples' habits and innovating our own methods in order to refine our creative output. This level of detail almost requires that someone old guides you in the process. Luke had Yoda. Frodo had Gandalf. Harry had Dumbledore. Eragon had Brom. Notice this universal pattern in fictional stories. Their structure is largely the same, while the content is different.

This is the same for our lives in general. We all are operating by the same rules of time and energy. The structure of life is similar, the specific story is what makes you special. Anyways, ignoring that philosophical side note, psychologists define four steps to practicing deliberately.

(1) clearly defined stretch goal
(2) full concentration and effort
(3) immediate and informative feedback
(4) repetition with reflection and refinement

This type of activity really taxes the mind, which is why I don't do it often. World class experts can usually handle about 4 hours of deliberate practice a day. First, they consciously craft their habits and structure their lives around their purpose. Second, they pour more time and energy and intensity and passion and perseverance and motivation and purpose and hopeful optimism into this structure. They pour their souls, their essence and substance, into living a conscious life.

They saturate their brain and being with purpose. They practice and practice and refine and refine until what was once "conscious incompetence becomes unconscious competence". I don't think that we understand the mechanisms, but it seems gritty people that engage in deliberate practice are more likely to experience flow and meaningful and spontaneous engagement with their craft. Perhaps, these two processes are not so contradictory after all.

Remember, science proves that extrinsic goals—such as becoming filthy rich, beautiful, popular, and famous—do not truly lead to happiness due to hedonic adaptation. Intrinsic goals, goals tied to our most substantial values, are what really propel human performance. They're the only way that we're going to care enough to complete the 10, 000 hours.

15
Micro-Habits and Time

Micro-habits: daily actions requiring minimal input and effort that can end up radically transforming your life. A good micro-habit is waking up with gratitude every morning. A bad micro-habit is watching the morning news. One study with Ariana Huffington found that 3 minutes of negative news in the morning increases the chances of having a bad day by 27%, as reported by participants 6 hours later. In my life, I've made many mistakes and learned many lessons. Trust me when I say that one tiny but consistent act, for good or for ill, separates success from failure, wealth from poverty, and a flourishing life from suicidal depression.

So let's turn to the most difficult task in the book: the transformation of our habits. From personal experience, I can tell you that there's going to be much failure and backsliding, but don't give up. For two days, record every little action you take and every thought you think. Then connect each action with its consequence. Cause and effect. Is each action worth the time you invest? What is the opportunity cost of each action (that is, by taking one action, what other thing could you be doing with that time)? Does the action lead to happiness and self-improvement? Or does it lead to unpleasant or neutral consequences?

Now comes the tough part. You need to kill any habit that's not worth its given time value, and then consciously set up micro-habits that help you live happier. These are the little nudges, the tiny investments that pay out in huge dividends for the future. Here are a few micro-habits that will radically upgrade your life.

1. Listen to audio-books in your car to develop skill sets

2. Journal Your Thoughts and Aspirations

3. Do Mini-Meditations Throughout the Day.

4. Drink Healthy Fruit-Veggie-Protein Smoothies

5. Meditate in the Morning.

6. Learn High Intensity Interval Training.

7. Start the day with clarifying questions.
What are my tasks/goals for the day? What are my priorities?

It is these types of mini-rituals, applied day in and day out, that turn one man into a success and another into a failure. Just study the people around you. Find out what a person does daily, and I can tell you whether he is healthy and happy or sick and sad. Okay. Now we've chosen some good habits, but remember that this is just part of the fun. Probably the most important habit, what I call the master habit, is time management because successfully managing your time naturally optimizes every other micro-habit.

"Your focus is your reality." - Yoda

16
Self-Mastery

How important is self-control, focus, and willpower? Let's consider the social implications. Divorce. Domestic Violence. Drug Abuse. Depression. Suicide. Many studies show that these problems stem from inner failures as much as outer conditions. Conversely, when analyzing what qualities lead to a happy life, scientists put self-control at the top of the list. One rigorous study followed one thousand children over thirty years, finding that the children rated as having the highest self-control were more likely to have better health, happier marriages, and higher paying jobs as adults. Meanwhile, children judged to have the lowest self-control ended up with a 40% criminal conviction rate by the age of thirty-two. They predicted the future decades in advance just by assessing self-control.

These findings are pretty scary. So what can we do about it? The answer is quite a lot. Willpower, to oversimplify, is the conscious manipulation of one's natural tendencies. Like a muscle, it is a store of psychological energy that tires from use, but it can be strengthened by practice. While willpower is essentially an inside job, outer conditions matter if you want to get the most out of this limited substance.

Sometimes, money boosts willpower. People tap into willpower reserves they never knew they had when you provide some financial incentive. Another tactic is to change your environment. For many experiments, scientists have to rigorously control for environmental stimuli because the smallest things have the largest impact on our behavior. For example, the cleanliness of science labs alters the decision-making of subjects. Clean rooms lead to greater self-control and healthy food choices. Dirty places do the opposite. Finally, the best way to boost self-control is to just practice, day in and day out.

Self-control is not about harnessing huge bursts of willpower to get stuff done. It is about having daily habits. It is about using your top down conscious mind to program routines into your bottom up habit forming unconscious. Those with willpower do not necessarily have "power" per say, but stamina. Maybe, we should call it un-will-stamina. High will individuals have self-control because they don't expend their precious willpower on things that drain the average person. For them, exercise is an automatic habit. Reading is a habit. Working is a habit. Kindness is a habit. Calmness is a habit. Happiness is a habit. Little efforts everyday build the control that we so desperately need in our lives. In one study, two weeks of working on your posture was shown to significantly boost self-control. Another study found that reaching your goals in one area of life naturally translates into more discipline in other areas. So disciplined eating translates into disciplined studying, which translates into disciplined exercise and so on and so forth.

So what is the ultimate message of this section? That you can change? That you have the power? That you need to get your life together? No! Well, yes...but the really big point is this: Since willpower is a limited substance, take this whole self-development thing slow. Relax! Forgive yourself for being an idiot. Improve little by little. Focus on transforming one habit at a time. I'll end with an activity. Look at your life right now. Determine what needs to change. What areas are bad right now? What can you improve upon? Choose the one failing of yours that is the most disastrous to your happiness, health, and life goals. Work on changing that habit. Save the other stuff for later. Let's end the section with some mini-facts about focus.

Qualities of Focus

(1) Willpower Depletes Over Time— old habits and laziness tend to take over as the day progresses.

(2) Focus Means Control — Depression, anxiety, and other such maladies often occur because individuals are unable to command their thoughts, to laser in on one task and stay at that task until it is done. Or vice versa, people are unable to drop a task that is useless (like chronic worrying), and shift focus towards something enjoyable.

(3) Focus Means Synchrony — Your brain is firing more or less in harmonic fashion when focus is laser-like. But if your mind is filled with chaotic thoughts, this synchrony disappears and MRI's of your brain tell the same story as your thoughts. A person's mind usually wanders 20 to 40 percent of the time during reading.

More Wandering = Less Comprehension.

"This optimal brain state for getting work done well is marked by greater neural harmony; a rich, well-timed interconnection among diverse brain areas." ~ Daniel Goleman, Focus

Ways to Cultivate Focus

(1) Cultivate Meta-Cognition (i.e. meditate) — Remember, meta-cognition is the ability to reflect on our thoughts. It is thinking about thinking. That way, we can look inside our heads and nudge our thoughts in the direction we desire.

(2) Ultradian Stages — These are the 90-120 minute cycles that we go through during sleep and during the day. What this means is that we're exceptionally focused for the one to two hours in the morning after we wake up. Then we experience a cyclic dip for about 20 minutes, during which we feel lethargic and find it difficult to focus.

(3) When you experience this dip, psychologists suggest mental relaxation activities such as meditation, music, socializing, taking a power nap (apparently, 20 minutes is the ideal length for power naps), and going for a walk and communing with nature.

(4) Called "attention restoration therapy" by Stephen Kaplan of U Michigan, it was experimentally determined that walking in nature leads to better focus on later tasks than things like video games, the internet, and even walking down a city street. Why? Because in nature, you don't find people shouting and arguing and acting like monkeys generally. Trees do not place demands on our attention.

> "Mastering others is strength,
> mastering yourself is true power."
> ~ Lao Tzu

17
Goal Setting

"What you get by achieving your goals is not as important as what you become by achieving your goals."
~Henry David Thoreau

Goal - an aim or outcome towards which one directs one's thought and action.

Motivation - a psychological impulse that elicits passion and persistence towards achieving one's goals.

These two factors are so tied together that it is impossible to have the second without the first. Dozens of studies show that self-conscious goal setting results in greater happiness, drive, wealth, social status, and success in life. One study performed on struggling college students found that a four month goal setting program increased their grades by 30% compared to the control group. The program taught them how to set realistic, challenging, meaningful, and specific goals. It also showed students how to develop detailed strategies for achieving those goals. Another study by Dr. Gail Matthews followed 267 people and found that those who regularly wrote down their goals, created action plans, and shared their dreams with a friend were 42% more likely to achieve their goals compared to those that occasionally thought about them.

So what is going on here? Basically, goal setting changes you by changing the flow of your thoughts. They begin to focus on the distant future. In one experiment, heroin addicts and a control group created a story about a guy named Bill. Specifically, the subjects imagined what Bill's thoughts were when he woke up in the morning. On average, Bill's thoughts ranged over nine days for the heroin addicts, while they stretched to four and a half years in the control group. In other experiments, it was found that high income participants looked even further into the future.

Study after study shows that kids with long term objectives (find a wife, get a good job, etc.) frequently do better in school. So you might want to start thinking about your future, right? Let's do it right now. Take a minute. Ponder where your life is heading. Think about where you will be in one year...in five years...in ten? I'll be here when you get back....Okay, done pondering? Now stop. Focus on the next few weeks. While long term goals are valuable, short-term goals are what get the job done. Studies comparing groups of students show that short-term goals increase performance way more than long-term goals. Small steps make the journey. So let's put this stuff to practice.

1. Set a valuable goal.

2. Consider long-term benefits. Set short-term standards.

3. Monitor your progress. Write about it. Then, adjust and recommit to your goal.

4. Reward yourself for little successes, and really party hard for the big ones.

So far, we've been floating in the realm of abstract thought. We want to make this stuff raw and emotional. We want to tap into your passions. To do this, you can use creative visualization. This technique uses imagination to elicit fear and desire as you imagine the worst consequences of making bad decisions and the great benefits of making good ones. Let's say you set yourself a goal to study before a test. Imagine this. If you party before the test, you can flunk out of college and get stuck in McDonalds for the rest of your life. Really imagine yourself in this situation. Think of the smell of flipping burgers, the feeling of having no money and no wife, and being tired and broke at the age of 40. Then, imagine the results of making good decisions like graduating college, finding a hot wife, and getting a great job. Feel the respect of your peers and family. Imagine a job that fills you with happiness and purpose. Think of the nice house and fancy vacations.

Of course, life will probably give you something in between these two scenarios, but every action you take will draw you towards one future and away from the other. To conclude, goals maximize happiness, minimize pain, and have a deep effect on the individual striving towards them.

18
Garden of the Mind

The quality of your thoughts determines the quality of your life. What you think is who you are. It matters whether your thoughts are creative, novel, rich, and positive, or whether they are repetitive, dull, and negative. And thoughts are self-moving creations. Once you plant a seed within the mind, that thought-seed grows to influence the direction of your life. The mind is truly like a garden. It takes effort and time to plant flowers and pull weeds. If you do not control your thoughts, then they have a habit of growing out of control. Instead of you using the mind, the mind uses you.

They say that a life of purpose is the purpose of life. But finding meaning in life is purely an internal process. If you think meaningful thoughts, then your life will become meaningful. If you think happy thoughts, then life will be happy. Reality becomes what the mind makes of it. So let's make reality meaningful by creating meaning in your life right now. Here are three questions:

What productive task do I love to do?

Simple question. Very difficult to answer. The first step to finding meaning is tapping into your passions. And remember, these have to be *your* passions; not some ideas that society has foisted upon you. So what do you love to do? What is something you would create or study or work on even if no one paid you to do it?

What does the world need?

The second question to meaning involves looking at the world with all of its problems and challenges, and seeing whether you can do something about any of them. Try connecting your passion with the needs of others.

What am I willing to get good at?

The third question is all about quality. People will not like what you give them unless it has value. In order to create value, you have to practice your passion until you get good at it. All of these questions become easier to answer once you change the relationship between you the thinker and your thoughts. Instead of thoughts unconsciously running through the mind, the thinker should consciously plant seeds, replacing negative and dull thoughts with positive and fruitful ones. How does one do this?

There are two strategies that can update your patterns of thought. The first is through positive affirmations. You update your thoughts by updating your self-image. Often, people have negative self-talk running their inner dialogue. Instead, they should repeat positive mantras to themselves such as "I am disciplined, energetic, and happy." If you say these types of things to yourself a few hundred times, then you cannot help but believe them.

The second way involves creating an ideal self. Take time to think about your best possible self. By doing so, you push your mind to think in novel and creative ways. If you consistently visualize yourself becoming a great doctor or lawyer, then the mind will naturally work to make that vision a reality. You cultivate optimism for your future, which naturally bends your thoughts towards happy and productive directions.

"The mind is its own place, and in itself can make a heaven of hell, a hell of heaven.." John Milton

19
Habit Formation

The power of beliefs, of ideas, of continuous learning, on our habits is difficult to determine exactly, but recent advances in the psychology of the unconscious shows that it's much more powerful than we once believed. Our systems of living are largely determined by our models of reality. Habits, or repeated patterns of behavior, are initially the result of cultural and social influence. They are unconsciously carried out well into adulthood. Do you know about the rat-maze-chocolate experiment? As the rats ran the maze faster and faster, their brains actually stopped working as hard. They went quiet as the ancient basal ganglia took over and turned new behaviors into automatic habits.

When programmed unconsciously, our habit forming brain is liable to drive our "decisions", our lives, and human civilization in general back into the dark ages. On the flip side, if we plug conscious self-awareness into the equation, the power of our lower brain machinery can be unleashed to optimize our lives and create a future of goodness for generations to come. How do we do this? How do we save the world? We create rituals. We create rituals for everything. The most successful people, the scientists and innovators pushing this world forward, are creative precisely because they have programmed optimal rituals into their habit forming brains. Focus is limited.

Self-discipline will only take you so far. But habits, once formed, are easy to maintain and pay off in huge dividends for the rest of your life.

So how do we create rituals? Tal Ben Shahar explains the process like this: "Building rituals requires defining very precise behaviors and performing them at very specific times — motivated by deeply held values." And that is what we're going to do for the rest of this section. We're going to structure our lives and create systems of living that allow us to do more in less time to be happier and more successful. There is a simple two step process to update both our models of reality and systems of living.

The Discovery Process

First, you have to look at your life and see if you're living according to your deepest values, greatest potential, and most awesome life path. Then you have to read a lot of somewhat legitimate sources in order to find out what is scientifically, or least popularly, proven to work. Here are some steps to do that.

1. Read loads of books on psychology and personal growth.
2. Prime the brain into creative thought by becoming happy.
3. List the thought-habits and activity-habits that might make you happier, smarter, and healthier.
4. Apply to your life diligently for 21 days

5. Determine which habits make you happy now and set you up for happiness in the future.

Refresh and Feedback

Again, I want to emphasize that much of the suffering in this world is created by centuries old systems of living. Imagine the untapped creative potential of entire continents in our world today. Our job as humans, the most creative and adaptive species on earth, is to consistently step back and rethink our systems of living, both for the individual and for human civilization in general. So here are some steps required to update your systems of living.

1. Recognize changing needs and problems.
2. Find role models.
3. Look for continuous feedback, both positive and negative.
4. Ask if this new habit or belief is making you happier or healthier.
5. If it is, then do it more. If it isn't working after a couple weeks, then try something new.

Over time, you'll find your optimal habits and be able to separate good systems from better from best. An incredible thing starts happening if you stick to optimal living for long enough; you experience what the Japanese call, Kaizen, a perpetual (and often accelerating) state of growth.

20
Blissipline

Good Goals —> Happy Now = Awesomeness

Blissipline. I love this word. It means the discipline of happiness. It implies that happiness is a worthwhile pursuit for both science and for society. And it implies that happiness is a project requiring discipline and effort. So how do you create a blissipline? You take some of the brightest minds in America, give them some money and free time, and then have them apply rigorous methods to determine, objectively, what actions and beliefs create happiness. Positive psychology, the science of happiness, has taught us many things about ourselves, but perhaps the most important is the power that good goals have over our decisions and, consequently, our happiness. In what is perhaps the best thought of Vishen's book, The Code of the Extraordinary Mind, he breaks happiness into three categories.

1. Happiness from Special and Unique Experiences
2. Happiness from Growth and Awakening
3. Happiness from Meaning

Why is this breakdown so great? 1. Comprehensive simplicity. 2. It highlights the importance of goals as a guide to decision making and the good life. Without the right goals, and without a good plan to get there, these three sources of happiness are entirely beyond our reach. And again, the right goals depend on having the right values. And the right values depend on not confusing means goals with end goals. Since our primate heritage has biased our decisions towards material considerations over what truly matters (joy, love, and meaning), we are, quite literally, enslaved to the extrinsic factors of motivation (money, acceptance, or prestige).

Many psychologists have shown that this slavery often results in suffering down the road. For their article titled "The Dark Side of the American Dream," Richard Ryan and Tim Kasser interviewed groups of college kids and then showed that those who put money at the center of their lives were less likely to be healthy, happy, and self-actualized.

Another experiment at the University of Rochester examined the flip side of the equation, showing that students driven by purpose goals over profit goals reported higher levels of well-being and life satisfaction up to two years after college. What's more, they derived pleasure from the knowledge that they were slowly reaching their goals; forget the fact of attaining them. Meanwhile, when psychologists interviewed the profit driven kids and followed up two years later, they found that those who had attained their money and status goals were no happier than two years earlier. Imagine what it was like for the money driven students who failed to get what they wanted. Such studies highlight certain insights that religions hit upon ages ago. If you tie your happiness to things beyond your control, they invariably end up making you happy or sad depending on the vagaries of fate.

Extrinsic goals create conditional happiness. Moreover, they create belief-sets built upon that conditionality. So long as you tell yourself that you won't be happy until so and so, or that you can't be happy when so and so happens, you brainwash yourself into creating self- fulfilling prophecies. Your expectations often create your reality, for better or for worse.

So what am I saying? That you need to go Buddha-mode and live homelessly happy? No. Other studies show that money loving students really do end up making more money than the purpose driven idealists. I'm sure that this connection becomes stronger as you become smarter and grittier. And nobody's telling anybody to give it all up. It takes all kinds of folks to build a happy world. And indeed, when money is relegated to its proper place, when it comes naturally as a result of pursuing your intrinsic growth oriented goals, it really does make life and the world a better place. For example, money provides for novel experiences. It frees up time. It allows you to help others. Money creates happiness so long as it's used properly.

21
The Best Kind of Goal

In Happier, Tal Ben Shahar talks about the ideal type of goal, the Self-Concordant Goal, which stems from one's deepest values and interests. Passion. Altruism. Purpose. When you strive to unfold the qualities that are natural and good and unique to you, the desire for status takes a back seat to intrinsic, meaningful, and self-driven goals. In order to set these goals, you need both a high degree of autonomy from social forces, and a prolonged process of self-inquiry. You must tap into your deepest impulses, desires, and passions. Only then can you create goals that set your soul on fire. You know what I mean, right? Goals that create flow experiences. Goals that, when you're working towards them, fill you with this deep sense of contentment and, in that rare moment, total and mind blowing euphoria and elation. This is what altruistic, purpose filled goals give to us. People treat the Buddha and other spiritual folks as though they're making some huge sacrifice. On some occasions (Jesus comes to mind), this is undoubtedly true. But in another paradoxical sense, being selflessly aligned with something greater is the most selfish thing you can do for yourself. As Tal Ben Shahar says, "The proper role of goals is to liberate us, so that we can enjoy the here and now." Think about your own pyramid of time and doing things. When consciously crafted, it brings structure, coherence, and direction to your life. It works so that the smallest actions are imbued with meaning and significance.

22

The Mating Game

Perhaps no part of human behavior is more determined by the unconscious than our desire for mates and children. These drives are so fundamental to our survival that we have evolved instincts of super-sensory brilliance to carry them out. For example, did you know that when men rated the photos of women for attractiveness (some of whom had dilated eyes and others who did not), these men unknowingly rated the women with dilated eyes as being more attractive? When asked why they chose these women, the men came up with all kinds of reasons other than the women had large pupils. Why is this the case?

Because physiology tells us that women's eyes dilate when attracted or sexually aroused. It makes sense from an evolutionary perspective. The men or women who instinctively act upon this knowledge would be more successful in propagating children. Even though we aren't aware of it, eons of evolution have inserted this program into our genomes. It is a trait determined by biological factors, like the trait of attraction itself. If a good looking lady even looks at a guy, his brain gives him a shot of the pleasure inducing molecule, dopamine.

And though there is undoubtedly overlap between men and women, there does seem to be a difference in the way each sex falls in love. When placed under an fMRI, the visual and sexual areas of men's brains light up as they look at a photo of their significant other. Meanwhile, women's brains process their lover through the lens of memories and attention. Such biological distinctions appear to have an evolutionary basis as well. While men, who could theoretically father hundreds of babies with dozens of women, pursue women exhibiting signs of beauty and fertility, women, who must care for their children, look for men with clear signs of power and wealth. Even the male voice matters to women, since it signals his virility and testosterone levels. When asked to rate men's voices for attractiveness, they rated deeper voices as being more attractive.

The female mating play book revolves around these kinds of rational calculations, of whether a man is willing to commit, and whether he is willing to invest in the children he sires with her. Meanwhile, the male playbook just wants to have a connection with the best looking lady that will have him. (Men are particularly attracted to the hourglass body ratio.) Such is the name of the game. This is the power of the animal unconscious within us. Indeed, our subconscious is so powerful that good looking people end up getting higher salaries, better jobs, and even lighter jail sentences than their less attractive fellows.

It stinks for "ugly" people that the initial stages of a relationship are so deeply founded upon animal attraction. Fortunately, these things disappear once the human side takes over. When people are asked what trait is most important in a potential lover, kindness comes out at the top of the list. Being supremely self-confident is also a must. One's mental state subconsciously affects one's tone of voice, posture, and emotions. These below the surface behaviors are more significant than the words one uses. Words account for about 7 percent of the emotional meaning of a message. Studies show that even if you are delivering a negative statement, your tone of voice and posture end up being the main determinant of whether the other person perceives it as such. So if you approach a woman or man you like with positive energy, a smile, and some confidence, you are more likely to prime the other person's unconscious to respond positively as well.

If you really really like someone and they don't like you in return, you can use the strategy of priming to up your chances. One experiment with college age guys showed that if they see a girl more frequently, they rate her as being better looking.. This is called the exposure effect. Nevertheless, don't hang around too much. Another study showed that if a guy is given a brief glimpse of a girl, as opposed to a long time studying her picture, the briefly glimpsed girl is reported as being more attractive. Women show this tendency as well, but guys are more easily manipulated because they're so sexual and visual.

Now guys, a similar dating study provides us with a strategy when we're asking a girl out. Researchers in France had a group of good looking young guys ask random girls out on a date. With one group of women, they lightly touched them on the arm during their proposal (a very light touch, the women didn't even notice it). The other group was not touched at all. Besides this difference, the nature of the proposal was the same. Same words, same demeanor, etc. So what was the conclusion of the study? The light arm touch doubled the men's chances of success. 20% success rate vs. 10%. Also, you want to make your proposal in a positive setting. People tip waiters more money when it's sunny outside. Their behavior changes in all kinds of subtle ways. So you might want to wait until the sun is out before you ask a girl out.

Now ladies, we have another strategy when it comes to dating. Basic lesson in male psychology: we like danger. We like a little pizzazz. Researchers conducted a study on whether the environment influences a man's willingness to pursue a woman. The answer: yes. When an attractive woman was recruited to ask random guys to fill out a questionnaire, those interviewed on a low and safe bridge were much less likely to pursue a second date with her than those interviewed on a high, slightly moving bridge hundreds of feet in the air. After the interview, the lady gave out her contact information in case the guy had any questions. 2 of the 16 safe bridge participants called her, while 9 of the 18 men on the anxiety inducing bridge called her. Think about it, ladies. Getting a guy's heart rate up doesn't require that you sleep with him. Just use a fun and interesting date to get his body (and therefore unconscious) primed for excitement.

23

Falling in Love

Alright, you did it! Using the help of a bunch of psychologists, you have succeeded in attracting and retaining the mate of your choice. You are in love perhaps. Or maybe not yet. Testing the waters is finicky business. This section is designed to deepen your love. It will help you find out if the guy is for keeps, or whether he should be kicked to the curb. As mentioned, women and men both prefer partners that are kind and compassionate; those who consistently consider the emotions and perspective of the other. This basic competence is the bread and butter of every real relationship, and this is where most guys miss the mark. They focus only on sex and looks when they should be focusing on the human being inside. This transition is described by philosophers as going from I-It to the I-You. The body is the it. The feeling human is the you.

When we connect to the human in another, we are more likely to generate what scientists call rapport. Couples in rapport synchronize their thoughts and feelings. Interactions are natural, smooth, and positive, naturally implying a level of cognitive and emotional empathy. You just know what the other person thinks and feels. When you smile, they smile. When you feel love, they feel love.

This capacity for union through synchronous emotions, thoughts, and behavior appears to stem, as usual, from our unconscious need to be loved. And naturally, the need to be loved ties in with an unconscious form of self-love. Have you ever heard that tale about how married couples start looking like each other? It actually might be the other way around. One study looking at fifteen thousand public marriages found that people get married to people who share the same first letter of their first name. This also connects to looks. People marry reflections of themselves, a psychological thing called implicit egotism.

This similarity strengthens bonds between lovers. If you are of similar intelligence, looks, and personality, then your relationship is more likely to turn into love. You achieve rapport more easily. Since emotions are incredibly contagious, you attune to the physiological state of the other. (Meditating together is a great way to bond with a lover. It has to do with the parasympathetic state that it puts you in. You engender loving feelings more easily when you're relaxed.) Remember, our social connections are powerful determinants of health and happiness. They can either boost our moods or drag us into misery.

As such, we need to recognize the dualities inherent in our closest, most intimate relationships. There are two of you trying to become one. It's not always easy. The male is almost always bigger and stronger. The female is almost always more aware. Love arises when these power imbalances are remedied to the greatest extent possible. Power and powerlessness, unfortunately, has been the way of the world for most of human history. Men=Power. Women=Powerlessness. The conscious relationship tries to remedy this imbalance.

Finally, and this is the most important reason for understanding the power/powerlessness aspect of relationships, falling in love requires a deep awareness of who sets the tone of social interactions. In an experiment where an emotionally expressive partner was set up with an emotionless one, it was usually the case that the emotional one transferred his or her emotions into the emotionless one. This is great when the powerful person is always happy. It sucks if the emotional person is depressed or worse. Therefore, falling in love requires that we be aware of the emotions passing between lovers, and that we consciously modulate those emotions so the expressive one becomes happy or the happy one becomes expressive.

24

On Being an Awesome Husband or Wife

Alright! Congratulations! Using this book, you found the one that you want to spend the rest of your life with. Most traditional cultures desire that you get married now. Sign that contract! Ball and chain! While I definitely understand the reasons, the divorce rate in America requires that we be more cautious before we tie the knot. Psychologists tell us that passionate love must run its course before we can truly know if we love someone.

It's been discovered that passionate love is like a drug, producing similar effects to heroin or cocaine. There is a tiny part of the brain that, when lovers look at each other, explodes with pleasure and caring that ends up becoming an addiction. Sex is a drug. Lovers literally become one with each other. Sex seems to triple the level of oxytocin in a man's brain. Since females have up to seven times more oxytocin than males (which remember relates to caregiving, attachment, and love), frequent sex aligns the brains of both lovers.

Passionate love is highly intense and emotional. Fantasies, idealization, and sexual arousal mark the beginning of most romantic relationships. When you first start dating and during your first years of marriage, research shows that your head is at a very different place than it is once those fiery embers cool down. One day if you're lucky, your passionate love will turn into companionate love. Each is a different process associated with different behaviors, and success in marriage involves effectively navigating from one form of love to the other.

A famous study found that marriage does boost levels of life satisfaction, but for only two years or so, after which people fall back to their prior levels of happiness. And this time frame applies to love as well. It takes two years for passionate love to run its course, and the loss of this love seems to be a powerful factor as to why many relationships end in divorce. Marriages built around passionate love burn bright for a little while and then fade just as quickly, while marriages based on companionship do the very opposite. Companionate love grows with time because it requires time and effort to grow.

Companionate lovers describe each other as respectful, caring, loyal, and friendly as opposed to the sexual "can't get enough" attitude of passionate lovers. Passionate love focuses on the I-It relationship, while companionate love focuses on the I-You. And while it seems you can have passionate and companionate love together (in fact, they can even strengthen each other), they each come from very different forms of thinking. One is driven by instinctual desire. The other arises from conscious choices about commitment and intimacy.

But commitment doesn't automatically make a woman happy. You have to understand the different psychologies of men and women. Study after study has shown that women do things differently. From communication to the way they think to the things they do, women prize bonding and interdependence more than men do. In one study of 264 couples, the most important part of a relationship for women is how well the couple communicates, while men tend to enjoy activities with their significant others.

And while men seek simple solutions to problems in relationships, women are less goal oriented. For them, communication isn't about finding problems and solving them. It's about processing emotion and gaining a deeper understanding of the relationship. One quality of highly successful marriages comes from understanding the wisdom of feminine psychology. When you talk about things only when problems come around, then you're more likely to associate "relationship talk" with negative emotions. Instead, you should talk about the relationship at all times. There's a famous marital term called "partner affirmation", which is the practice of validating your partner's emotions, feelings, and goals. Science has found that, more important than being a shoulder to cry on, successful relationships are defined by how well couples process positive emotions together. According to the researcher Shelly Gable, there are four ways to respond to good news. Imagine your wife tells you that she got a promotion at work. How would you react?

(1) There's the active destructive way. "You got a promotion? Why? You're barely competent at cooking, much less high level sales."

(2) There's the passive destructive. "You got a promotion? Oh yeah. Well, I just got a bigger one the other day."

(3) There's the passive constructive. "Oh, that's great, honey." and go back to reading the newspaper.

(4) But the best way is the active and constructive way. That is, you respond to your partner's happiness with even more genuine happiness. Be like, "Oh, you got a promotion? That's totally sweet! We're gonna be rich one day. When did you get it? Where?" So notice the two qualities here: (1) You affirm your partner and a share in her happiness. This is the emotional side. (2) You build up your partner and ask her about the happiness creating situation. This is the social side.

Your life partner is the strongest determinant of your health and happiness. Social neuroscience tells us that our social relationships sculpt the wiring of our brains, conditioning the release of chemicals and stress hormones. Bad relationships are literally toxic to the body, while good relationships boost health. And the stronger the emotional connection between two people, the greater this force. Positive feedback loops of emotions form between husband and wife that can quickly spiral upwards into happiness, or downwards into toxicity and despair.

Through rigorous studies, researchers have found that it is the moment to moment emotional energy of interactions that determine how long relationships will last. Indeed, scientists have found an exact ratio of positive to negative moments that predict the future of relationships. For any relationship to last, you need three positive interactions to one negative interaction. For the relationship to be healthy and growing, you need a ratio of five to one. Most couples who rate their marriages as happy have five to one ratios.

Though simple, the positive vs. negative spectrum is an incredibly powerful scientific tool for measuring relationships. The researcher, John Gottman, was able to predict with 90% accuracy whether a couple would soon break up by simply observing their normal interactions. What's powerful is how specific he gets in his observations. He not only looks for positive vs. negative emotions, but the types of emotions displayed on the faces of couples. One emotion that was an immediate red flag signaling a doomed marriage was the emotion of contempt. You can't get much more negative than contempt.

And when it comes to positive emotions, it's laughter that binds couples together the tightest. In fact, one study found that not laughing with your significant other is more indicative of whether a marriage will fail than not having sex. So how do you keep your marriage strong? Laugh together. Find the funny side of life. Laughter is the bread and butter of social connection. It forms an instant bond between two brains and ties people tighter than anything physical.

To conclude, love is one of the highest aspirations of the human race, and marriage is a concrete symbol of that aspiration. Perhaps, no realm of human endeavor deserves more of our attention than the realm of marital relations. This section can be boiled down to three simple strategies for living a happy married life.

(1) Marriage is not about passion, but companionship.
(2) Marriage is a process requiring conscious effort and time.
(3) Marriage is about small and simple everyday interactions.

25

Dealing with Disagreement

According to John Gottman, 69% of problems in relationships have no quick fix. They are unresolvable, usually the result of different temperaments, preferences, and the basic struggles of everyday life. This fact tells us that it is pointless to tell couples not to fight. Disagreement is going to happen. It doesn't matter so much what couples argue about. And it doesn't really matter why. What matters is how couples go about airing their complaints to each other.

Again, this emphasis is necessary due to the differences between men and women. For example, in the beginning of most marriages, men are much more malleable in the eyes of their wives. They are more intimate, willing to talk about the relationship and whisper sweet nothings into the ear of their partner. But once passion turns into companionship, men change, preferring to do things with their wives instead of talk.

This is just one example of the difference between men and women. Another is the fact that women's biology tends to shift more during the ups and downs of marital relations. That is, women experience greater swings in heart rate, blood pressure, and stress hormone levels than men during both arguments and intimacy. Therefore, the responsibility falls largely on men to empathize and de-escalate tensions before we make our partners sick with anger and frustration. For example, researchers found that when men listen and empathize during disagreements as opposed to storming out of the room, wives experience lower levels of stress hormones.

And these small acts build up over time. How a couple manages conflict can be seen as a behavioral loop, reinforcing itself over time and many arguments. If a couple gets into the habit of not airing frustrations productively, this cycle can eventually ruin an otherwise healthy marriage. If, on the other hand, couples agree on the best way to disagree beforehand, then the marriage is well on its way to everlasting decency. For example, a bit of laughter injected into any argument lowers tension, allowing room for compromise and awareness. The ability to manage your partner's emotions, to de-escalate tensions and listen effectively, is the basis of what Daniel Goleman calls emotional and social intelligence.

Social intelligence is about having already decided guidelines to handle anything that may come up during a relationship. It's about creating a social contact ahead of time, knowing how to handle negative discussions and emotions when they do arise. So here's a contract I believe all couples need to tape to their fridge.

Contract for the Successful Marriage

(1) Be Open with Your Emotions - If you're angry, tell your partner that you're angry. If you're sad, then just be sad. Authenticity is essential to a healthy marriage. Let's not bury our resentments and annoyances. One study by Florida State University found that couples who openly display anger and air complaints end up being much happier in the long run.

(2) Take a Time Out - If either partner gets angry to the point of yelling or cursing, then the argument has progressed beyond the point of reason and needs to be put on hold. Anger is an emotion that has two phases: (1) the initial flare up and (2) the simmer period, which lasts for about half an hour afterwards. Instead of saying things in anger that you'll regret, why not wait until you cool down completely?

(3) Love the Sinner, Hate the Sin - It's important to realize that we're all human, that we all make mistakes, and that making a mistake doesn't mean that the partner's character needs to be called into question. Studies have shown that couples who directly attack their partner's personalities are more likely to divorce than couples who air complaints using the XYZ method. Instead of saying, "You forgot to do the dishes again! You are such a forgetful airhead," you should say, "When you did X (forgot to do the dishes), it made me feel Y (unappreciated), and I'd rather you do Z instead (not forgot to do the dishes instead).

(4) Listen More, Talk Less - Another indication of doomed marriages is when partners don't take the time to see things from another's perspective. Instead, they interrupt each other. According to John Gottman, whether a partner interrupted before the other could finish speaking was the most predictive pattern of whether a couple would break up. Most of these couples broke up within a year and half of the study.

(5) Doing Everything You Can to De-escalate Arguments - This means apologizing when you're wrong. It means empathizing with your partner's perspective, realizing that people are rarely one hundred percent wrong about anything.

(6) Celebrate the Good in Each Other - Gratitude for one another is essential to any marriage. It comes from not taking the other for granted. It arises through validation of your partner's goals, interests, emotions and dreams. Science has found that variety and novelty boost pleasure in relationships, so take the time to come up with new ways to appreciate each other. Write an appreciation letter to your lover. Try to bring out the ideal lover in the other instead of their less desirable qualities.

26

Making Awesome Children

Alright! You've navigated the twists and turns of dating, falling in love, and getting married. Your connection to your significant other has matured over the years and now you're ready to have children. This phase of life depends on the satisfaction of all prior phases. Happy children come from happy parents, and happy parents require happy marriages. It's all connected, and I would recommend not having children until you really grow to love your significant other as a companion. Give it a couple of years and see how you two feel about children. Since this act is likely the most important act you'll ever undertake, it should not be entered into lightly. You are bringing an experiencing, thinking, human being into this world, whose existence will not only influence your life but the lives of countless people that come into contact with your child.

Personally, I don't have children just as I don't yet have a wife, so I can't speak from personal experience. But after reading a decent amount of literature on parenting, I think there's one rule that makes for successful parenting: Be aware of just how impactful the smallest acts have upon your child's psychology. The first few years of life are when a toddler's brain grows to two thirds of its full size. The child's mind is a sponge, and research shows that how a parent interacts with their baby has deep and lasting consequences for the child. Parents determine their child's neural architecture. For example, one study looked at baby mice and found that the pups born to devoted mothers who licked and groomed them grew to have denser connections between their brain cells. Meanwhile, mothers who nurtured less created pups that learned more slowly.

The repetition of certain parental behaviors hundreds of times creates neural pathways in the mind of your child. As they grow into adulthood, children lose half of their neurons to a process called pruning. This is when unused neural pathways disappear, while consistently used neural pathways strengthen. Once they become set, it is tougher to change these linkages. But childhood is when these links are forming, so it is incredibly important to create neural pathways related to happiness and connection rather than depression and isolation. Once set, however, these behavioral pathways fire automatically, which means that if you fail to implant the right behavioral responses in your child at a young age, then those responses become automatic habits. The more you indulge in a habit, the stronger and thicker the neural pathways related to it become.

When they are babies, the child's mind is most flexible and open to neural programming. Neurogenesis, the creation of new neurons, is at its peak during childhood. And these new neurons mirror the mental processes of the adults around them. For example, the babies of depressed mothers are shown to have higher levels of stress hormones and lower levels of dopamine and serotonin. Similarly, children who experience consistent eye contact and loving behaviors from their parents regularly secrete neurochemicals related to pleasure and bonding. Children's brains reflect their environment. It's a scary thought, but there is a positive side. If children are consciously raised, this is an opportunity for parents to develop lifelong behaviors and habits in their child. Once the child grows older, their neural wiring becomes more rigid and therefore harder to change.

Teaching Social and Emotional Intelligence

Since children have more brain plasticity, childhood is the time to teach skills such as emotional and social intelligence. And these two capacities are closely related. One of the first lessons a child learns is how to distinguish between feelings. This ability to discover "how am I feeling?" fires the same part of the brain as "how is she feeling?" That is, the ability to know your own feelings helps you know another's feelings. Emotional and social intelligence foster empathy. To teach children this ability, teachers have used feeling face cards reflecting one of six basic emotions (joy, anger, sadness, fear, disgust, and surprise) in order to get kids talking about how they feel when they experience these emotions, and how to read these emotions in others. SEL (social and emotional learning) programs are shown to reduce misbehavior by 10 percent, increase good behavior 10 percent, and increase test scores. Change happens because you are shaping a child's brain on the neurological level. In brain scans, simply naming emotions is shown to calm the amygdala; the part of the brain responsible for emotions such as anger, fear, and sadness. It also controls aggression. Children able to calm the amygdala tend to be more popular and have an easier time forming social connections. The seven traits of emotional intelligence in a child are confidence, curiosity, intentionality, self control, relatedness, the capacity to communicate, and cooperativeness.

Singapore is the first country in the world to create SEL programs in every school. This country wide program can do things like lower crime rates and increase worker productivity. For example, one study showed that preschoolers taught self control have lower rates of teen pregnancy, school drop outs, and days of missed work. Another University of Washington study showed that parents with emotional intelligence, compared to those unable to handle their feelings, have children who show greater affection and who are more cooperative. These same five year olds had fewer behavioral problems and higher scores in math and reading.

28
Self-Control

Such studies show the extent to which small behaviors result in habits that determine the course of a person's life. Childhood is a window of opportunity to wire the right emotional and social habits. And the biggest teacher is the parent. Empathy in children, for example, is fostered by seeing how others react when someone else is distressed. If parents show care and concern, the child is likely to mimic that habit, while ignoring feelings results in maladjusted children. One way to foster empathy in the child is how the parent disciplines them. When a parent is benevolent and relies on reasoning, when the parent brings attention to how others feel instead of simply berating the child, this teaches them to show concern for others. Parents should bring attention to how a child's actions make others feel. And the parent should emulate these positive behaviors herself.

Children copy the adults around them. In one study, children watched one group of adults beat up a toy doll, while another group played with the doll quietly. Almost every child who saw the adult hitting the doll hit the doll himself. And when the adult played quietly with the doll, the child copied that behavior too. This study shows that self-control is a behavior that children acquire by imitation, and it is the most important quality that a parent ought to exhibit. Why?

Because study after study shows that self control determines the life of a child more than any other personality trait. One famous study on self-control is Walter Mischel's Marshmallow Experiment. In this study, children were given the choice between having one marshmallow now, or waiting ten minutes and getting two marshmallows in the future. Two groups of children were created from this setup. One group chose immediate gratification. The other opted to delay gratification. Afterwards, they followed these children through the years into adolescence. The results were astounding. They found that what these children chose at the age of four largely determined who they would become as adults. Those that chose immediate gratification were more likely to be juvenile delinquents, alcoholics, students with lower grades, and adults with unstable relationships.

Meanwhile, the children who waited for the two marshmallows at the age of four were more socially competent, effective, and better able to get into college and flourish. Another rigorous study followed one thousand children over thirty years, finding that the children initially rated with the highest self-control were more likely to have better health, happier marriages, and higher paying jobs as adults. Children judged to have the lowest self-control ended up with a 40% criminal conviction rate by the age of thirty-two. Again, the simple capacity for self-control determines the course of a person's life. The ability to delay gratification allows us to change our habits, which changes our brains.

Now, this research may have many parents throwing up their hands in frustration. After all, if a child's self control is determined at a very young age, then what can a parent do about it? The answer is quite a lot. Studies have shown that there are certain games and programs children can perform in order to increase their self-control. One preschool program specifically taught self control to its students, and found that these same preschoolers, when followed through the years, had lower rates of teen pregnancy, school dropouts, and delinquency. Other studies had kids play attention training games under an fMRI. Brain wave data indicates that just a few hours of such games shifts the neural activity of a child's brain towards her executive centers; brain wave patterns more frequently mirrored in adults.

So what are these self-control strategies? One involves constantly pointing out to kids the consequences of their actions. You don't simply discipline them, but draw their attention to the consequences of good behavior vs. bad behavior. Another strategy provides older children with the basics of CBT (or cognitive behavior therapy). Very simply, this program teaches kids about the relationship between their thoughts, feelings, and behaviors. It teaches kids how to alter their thoughts, and thereby change their feelings and behaviors. Children taught CBT are shown to have less anxiety and lower levels of pessimism and depression.

Conclusion

These are the basic methods you can use to create a healthy, happy, and awesome child. But remember, these methods ought to be applied creatively because no child is the same, and yet every child requires love. They deserve love. If you consistently apply this book to your life, you will end up creating an awesome child because everything is connected. If you have goals, discipline, happiness, and good habits on a personal level, these positive forces will combine to create a better marriage, a better family, and a better life.

The Habit Loop

cue → routine → reward → cue ("habit loop")

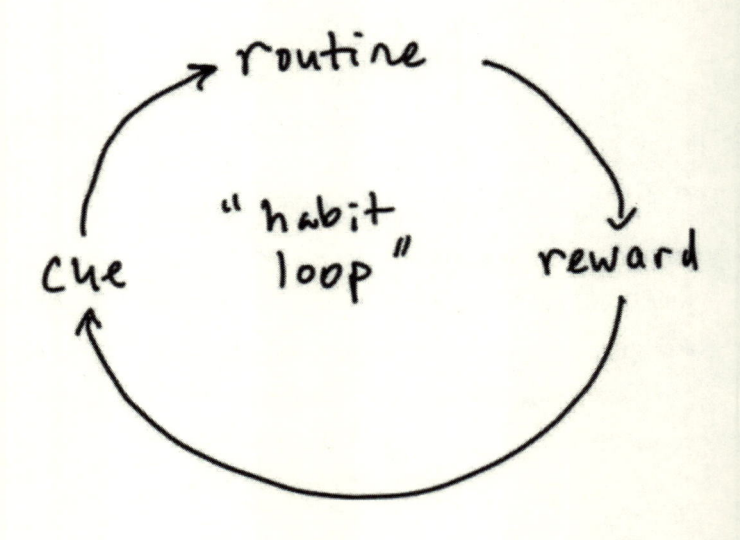

There are three components to the habit loop. First is the cue; the stimulus that triggers ancient regions of your brain to carry out an ingrained habit. The second is routine; the actual action or process engaged in. Finally, for any habit to stick, you need a reward; something telling your brain that the habit has value; that it is worth installing.

For this self optimization exercise, I want you to reflect on various habits that you have programmed into your brain either consciously or unconsciously (most likely unconsciously). Everyday you carry out hundreds of habit loops from brushing your teeth to eating junk food. Now, I want you to identify the most impactful habits that you have. These are the habits that you find significantly improve or worsen your life. Come up with and write down two good habits and two bad habits.

Now comes the fun part. Take these four habits and apply the habit loop to them. Consider the internal or external cue for your good habits. For example, the routine of exercise might be cued by the thought of your perfect future body. Or it might be the sight of fat people on the street. Or it could simply be seeing your gym clothes lying next to your bed. There are many cues for any one routine. There are also many variations of routine and many types of reward. The trick is to observe the qualities and variations of your habit loop for each habit. Take time to journal which habits you want to adopt or eliminate. In the next section, we go into how to change our habits.

Habit Transformation

Habits can be tough to create or destroy. You may think it is all about willpower or self-discipline. But while these qualities do have an impact on changing habits, they are not required to do so. All you need are smart tactics. Here are some major ways to tinker with the habit loop in order to make good habits stick and bad habits disappear.

(1)　　You can associate pleasurable rewards with good routines and consider the painful consequences of bad habits. For example, if you crave sugar and hate exercise, perhaps you can reward yourself after each workout with a healthy chocolate banana blueberry smoothie.

(2)　　You can alter your environment in order to create cues for good routines and get rid of cues for bad routines. So sticking with the exercise example, perhaps you can place your running shoes next to your bed. For bad habits such as junk food, you can simply hide the snacks in a tall cupboard and put the healthy options out in the open.

Motivation Equation

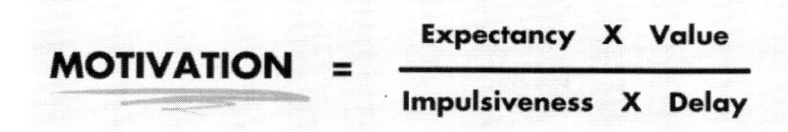

$$\text{MOTIVATION} = \frac{\text{Expectancy} \times \text{Value}}{\text{Impulsiveness} \times \text{Delay}}$$

For those of you who are not good at math, motivation increases when the numerator (the number above the line) increases and the denominator (the number below the line) decreases. If you want more motivation to reach your goals; if you want the necessary persistence and passion to overcome obstacles and push through the pain; then you need to understand how each of these terms applies to your life.

The first term is expectancy, or the expectation of success, or the level of confidence you have that you will reach your goal. You can increase this variable by using affirmations and altering the narrative you have in your head. The second term is value, or the level of importance that you place on your goal. You can increase this variable by reflecting on the positive consequence of achieving your goals. The third term is impulsivity, or your tendency to act without forethought and break your commitments. You can reduce this variable by practicing self-discipline and getting comfortable with being uncomfortable. Fourth, we have delay, or the time delay that exists between the now and reaching your goal. Motivation decreases when goals are too far off in the future. To decrease this variable, we need to break down our far off big goals into smaller bite size chunks. Mini-goals pave the way to reaching our dreams.

All of these forces play a role in shaping our level of motivation. And it is important to note that motivation changes as your goals vary in quality. High value goals tend to have a larger time delay and require greater discipline. They also tend to be harder to achieve, so you may not be as confident in achieving success. This is why so many people fail to shoot for their dreams. The prospects seem too daunting. And this is why understanding this equation is so essential; because, by tweaking each factor to the greatest of your ability, you give yourself a chance to really make great things happen.

Shifting Identity

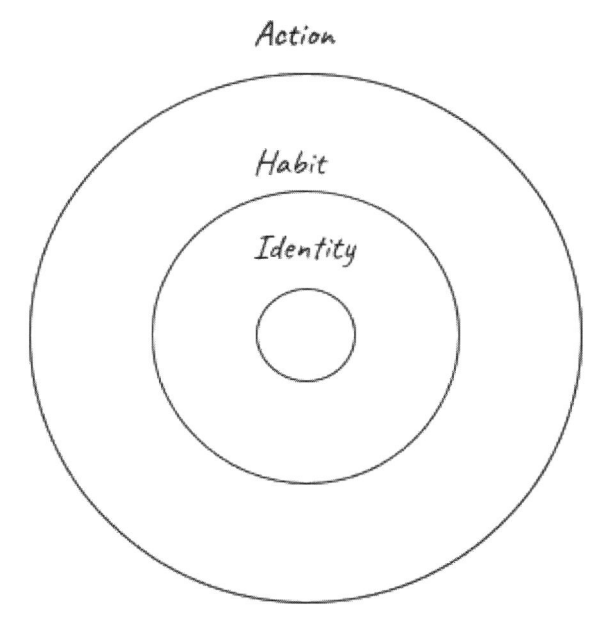

Action

Habit

Identity

Where does life transformation begin for you? Does it start from the inside out or the outside in? Let me explain. For most people, the idea of being in shape or successful or rich begins with the process of action turning into habits turning into your identity. This is why most people fail to create lasting change. They don't work on their core concept. They don't shift their identity first. If you need to see yourself achieve success in order to think of yourself as successful, then you have the equation backwards because you are depending on the external world to give you the validation that you can only give yourself.

Instead, try to think of yourself as the type of person who can easily achieve success or happiness. If your self identity is that of a depressed person, then it's going to be very hard to convince yourself that you can be happy. Your identity is your destiny. Use positive affirmations to work on your self-image and self concept. This isn't the image that you portray to the world. It is who you think you are on the deepest level.

And do not feel bad if you occasionally think lazy or depressed thoughts. These thoughts are not who you are as long as you don't identify with them. The second you get attached to your thinking is the second that you lose control of your identity and consequently your destiny. Work on thinking empowering and positive thoughts about who you are. Ask yourself what a successful person is to you and how a successful person thinks. Get very clear on your passions and life purpose. If you can easily answer the following questions, then you are well on your way to the life of your dreams.

(1)   What is success to you?
(2)   What are your passions and skills?
(3)   What kind of person do you see yourself as?

The Hero's Journey

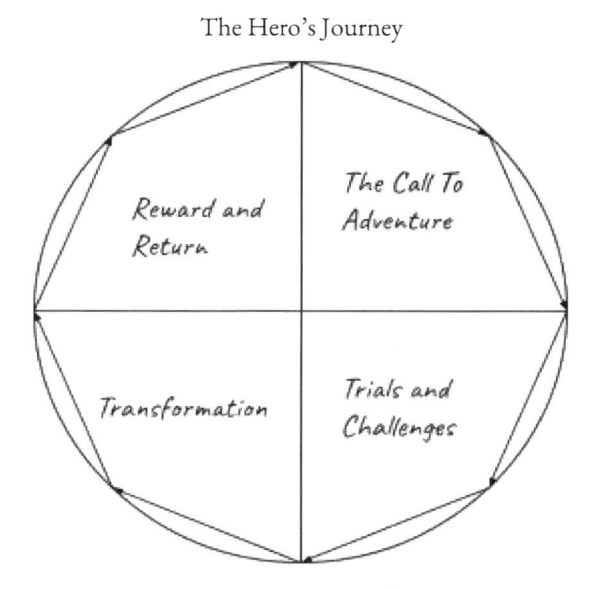

- Reward and Return
- The Call To Adventure
- Transformation
- Trials and Challenges

It is proven science that humans do not see the world as it really is. Instead, they see it as they are. Who you are determines the type of world you see. Your reality is determined by the stories you tell yourself about yourself and the world.

Who do you really see yourself as? Do you see yourself as a hero facing the challenges of life? Or do you just wake up without thinking about your purpose and go to the same old job with the same old people doing the same old thing? Do you desire to shoulder burdens greater than yourself to push the world in the direction of light and goodness? Or are you just trying to get through the day, focusing on your little life and pleasures to drown out the existential hole in your soul?

For ages, humans have created hero stories in order to fill the deep desire for meaning in their psyche. Carl Jung calls this deep psychic necessity an archetype. Just like every human has a heart and lungs, every human has a similar psychic (but unconscious) substructure generating their experience and the way they see the world. Why has the hero story shown up in dozens of civilizations around the world since the dawn of time? Because there is a hero archetype woven into the subconscious psyche of man.

This archetype imbues your life with meaning when you activate it. It engages the deep layers of the unconscious, so you feel passion for life and persistence in the face of challenges. It is all about the narrative that you build in your head about your life story and purpose. You can orient your life using the schema provided in the picture above. Apply the hero's journey to your life and see if you can make it fit. Let's go through it phase by phase.

(1)   The Call To Adventure - Have you found your passion and purpose yet? If so, then that is life calling you to fulfill your highest potential? Identify your calling and see how you can move towards it.

(2) Trials and Challenges - Every hero faces obstacles on the path to greatness. Identify the problem areas of your life and make a plan to solve them.

(3) Transformation - In every hero story, the hero must transform in order to grow and become his greatest self. The ability to evolve is your superpower. Use it.

(4) Reward and Return - Whether it is wealth, your soulmate, or any other reward, consider the positive consequences of achieving your potential for both yourself and the world.

Think about Harry Potter or Luke Skywalker. They faced many challenges and sacrificed a lot to achieve their purpose. They didn't go through life questioning whether it's worth living at all. The thought of meaning didn't even occur to them. They lived that meaning. This is your task as well. Change the narrative in your head. Think of yourself as a hero on the journey to transform yourself and the world. It's all about your perspective. It's about how you see things. Look at life like a hero and it will open up for you.

Micro Improvements, Maximal Results

Small Gains ⟶ Radical Change

Think about an ice cube. Everyday you show up in a cold room and turn the temperature up one degree. You wake up, walk to the room, turn the thermostat and leave. That ice cube will not stop being an ice cube until you hit 32 degrees fahrenheit. 31 degrees doesn't cut it. If you want the state to change, you have to hit the critical threshold.

Habits are a lot like an ice cube. They take time to cultivate and then they take time to manifest as results. For those who are unable to delay gratification, habit change can seem daunting. But the ice cube tells us that the desired result almost literally pops into existence when you put monthly effort into good habits. This is how the universe works. Things are not linear. There are breaks and curves and all kinds of things going on. Habits are one of those things. We don't realize that something is a habit until it has us in its grip. So let's be smart and think about our daily actions. Our habits either make us or break us. So commit to having the best habits in order to live the best life.

Get Specific

Habit Creation Exercise
I will perform behavior (x) at time (y) at the place (z).

When you're trying to upgrade your life, the goal is to (1) get specific on what your habits are, (2) determine the specific actions and habits you want to create and (3) make a specific plan to apply these new habits on a daily basis. Psychologists call this an intention to implement. You don't want to tell yourself, "I'm going to eat healthier." Instead, you want to detail exactly what healthy means to you. You want to write down the foods you're going to buy. You want to write down the meals you're going to cook. Make up a specific time and place that you're going to eat.

Science has shown that motivational literature does not work very well when it comes to changing habits. Instead, it boils down to the individual's willingness to get specific on their goals. Focus on the process of eating healthy more than the results of eating healthy. Focus on how you're going to do what you're going to do instead of why you're doing it.

36
Victim or Creator

There are two types of belief systems that play out in your life: the victim or the creator. The victim mentality has an external locus of control, meaning you believe that life is largely beyond your control and that things happen to you and not by you. The creator meanwhile has an internal locus of control, meaning you believe that you have power to influence and control your environment and life.

Studies have shown that whichever belief system you hold is the determinant of whether you are happy or not. Those who believe their lives are beyond their control have learned helplessness. They are more likely to be depressed, anxious, and unhealthy. Those who believe they can improve their situation have learned optimism. They are the ones more likely to workout, succeed, and flourish in life.

More foundational than this is the growth vs fixed mindset that we discussed earlier. You must realize that, no matter what your belief system is, you have the ability to change it. It is important that you apply the knowledge in this book because the process of gaining control over your life through habit formation is what's going to give you the level of control necessary for happiness.

How is habit formation connected to the idea of control? Because when you take time to master your body through exercise, your mind through reading, and your soul through meditation, you give yourself little doses of control. Slowly, your beliefs about yourself and the world will shift as you continue the journey of self development. You only have total control over one thing in your life, and that is yourself. So do yourself a favor and take control of it.

Models of Reality

Believed Truth + Passion + Action = Actual Truth

A belief about object x is what you think is true about object x. Your model of reality is the structure of your beliefs applied to either yourself or the world. Every belief you hold does not exist in isolation. They influence each other. They influence your reality. Beliefs are often unconscious. They influence every part of your life in ways that you do not see or understand. In one famous study, psychologists found that the expectations of researchers would influence the outcomes of the experiment.

For example, in one study, scientists were told that they had either smart rats or dumb rats. In reality, the rats were arbitrarily assigned these value judgments. In reality, they were all just rats. But this simple designation influenced the speed with which the rats ran the maze. The "smart" rats ran it faster simply because they were expected to run it faster.

Beliefs are self-fulfilling prophecies. Once you upgrade your beliefs about yourself, you upgrade your chances of achieving the life of your dreams. And there are two ways to change your beliefs. (1) You can change your behavior which in turn will change your beliefs about yourself. For example, if you run everyday for a year, then your belief about being lazy will disappear naturally. Or (2) you can change your beliefs and identity first, which will change your behavior. Both tactics play a role and even reinforce each other. The trick is to uncover your deep seated beliefs and change them to become a better version of yourself.

Actual Reality vs. Believed Reality

This book has shown you some of the studies surrounding the power of optimism and happiness. But let's be realistic. You can think positive all day, but if a crane lands on your head, you're toast. Reality has a way of blindsiding us when we're too optimistic. It's called naive optimism; a vision of the future built upon distorted perspectives of reality. Actual reality is not just sunshine and daisies. There are thunderstorms and rain too.

But this does not mean you give in to the dark side. Nothing kills your drive and passion more than thinking that your goals cannot be reached. That's why you need optimism alongside a healthy dose of realism. You need confidence alongside an awareness of the obstacles in your path. More than that, you need to be aware of the fact that believed reality can actually alter actual reality. It's called the placebo effect, and it doesn't just apply to the field of medicine. People who believe they are happy, successful, intelligent, and good looking are more likely to do better on tests, find good partners, and achieve more things in life. So what's the equation?

Optimism + Realism = The Good Life

Happiness and Excellence

I first encountered Shawn Achor when I saw him on YouTube, lecturing in this happiness class at Harvard. I was like, "This guy is really funny." And his book, The Happiness Advantage, is super useful for habit transformation. The basic formula is really simple. If you're happy on the inside, then it's easier to change bad habits and consciously structure your life. For the following sections, I briefly use Achor's words beside each principle to get us primed with intelligent writing, and then I summarize it for people on my level.

Quick Fact: Over 200 studies of 275, 000 people worldwide show that happiness optimizes every domain of life, like creativity, problem solving, work ethic, and job performance.

The Basics of Neuroplasticity — Your brain is super malleable, regenerative, and capable of total transformation.

"Indeed, if our thoughts, daily activities, and behaviors can change our brain, the great question becomes not if, but how much change is possible....we do not know the limits of human potential." ~ Shawn Achor

Happiness = Pleasure + Engagement + Meaning
~ Martin Seligman

Principle # 1 – The Happiness Advantage: "Because positive brains have a biological advantage over brains that are neutral or negative, this principle teaches us how to retrain our brains to capitalize on positive and improve our productivity and performance."

Emotional intelligence requires that we become happy first and successful second. It is only logical, since happiness leads to greater intelligence, motivation, and work ethic. Our emotions color our thoughts and alter the chemical composition of our brains. We produce dopamine, serotonin, and other chemicals when we're happy, which enhance both concentration and creativity at work. In one study, doctors primed to be happy were significantly faster and more accurate at diagnosing test patients. On the other hand, stress hijacks the creative spirit and creates a soup of toxic chemicals that circulate throughout the human body. Psychologists call it emotional hijacking, which happens when we're unable to use our prefrontal cortex to calm the limbic system. In a study by Richard Davidson, he found that those considered resilient and happy, when put in high stress situations (like solving difficult math problems under time pressure or writing about a traumatic experience), were much more likely to show greater activity in their prefrontal cortex relative to their limbic system.

In other words, happiness and resilience depend on your ability to control the stressed out amygdala, and this is done by consciously structuring your life. In the happy doctor experiment, do you know what made them dramatically better at creative thinking and accurate diagnosis? Do you know what made them happier? Candy. That's all it takes. The tiniest shots of happiness create big changes because they add up over time. Later, we discuss different ways to boost happiness. But for now, I like meditation the most. Studies show that meditation can totally restructure the brain resulting in permanent increases in self-awareness, empathy, and happiness. I recommend doing mini-meditations at work, which totally resets the brain when you're feeling overwhelmed.

But ultimately, I cannot tell you how best to optimize your work life. You have all the answers within you, young padawan. My job is to point out the opportunities for happiness and growth. With that end in mind, I'd like you to finish the following sentences. Get your creative juices flowing. This is the sentence completion test by Nathaniel Branden. I make up some of my own. Answer the questions quickly in order to bypass your rational mind.

(1) The things that make me happy are.....
(2) If I breathe deeply and allow myself to experience what happiness feels like...
(3) If I take more responsibility for my wants.....
(4) If I brought 5 percent more awareness to my life.....
(5) The small rituals that make me happiest during work are....
(6) The things that make me unhappy at work are....
(7) The small rituals that reduce stress at work are....
(8) The activities I lose track of time doing are...
(9) The activities that give me meaning, the feeling of going somewhere are...

40
Belief Creates Reality

Principle # 2 – The Fulcrum and the Lever: "How we experience the world, and our ability to succeed within it, constantly changes based on our mindset. This principle teaches us how we can adjust our mindset (our fulcrum) in a way that gives us the power (the lever) to be more fulfilled and successful."

Few people realize the degree to which belief transforms the brain. In one experiment, Japanese researchers told a group of blind-folded students that their right arms were being rubbed with poison ivy. In fact, the researchers had done no such thing. But the amazing thing is that all of the students' bodies reacted as though they had been rubbed by the actual poison ivy. Their arms were covered with rashes and boils. They were irritated and scratching like crazy. Then, these same students were rubbed on their other arm with real poison ivy, but the researchers told them that it was a harmless plant. Out of the 13 students, all who were found to be allergic to the substance, only two broke out with the rash.

How we see things doesn't just change our perception of reality; it bends reality itself as the world comes alive with opportunities, possibilities, and moments for enjoyment that you never would have seen had you not picked up this book. Inner happiness changes outer reality. Come on, Einstein taught us that things as absolute as time can be bent depending on the observer; so, how hard can it be to bend less absolute things such as your body or mind. If you can change the belief that your experience is fixed and immutable, then you will be amazed by how dramatically the world around you changes in response. Here's a simple equation to sum things up.

Growth Mindset + Goals + Social Support + Happy Goals + Health + Happiness + Incredible Belief in Oneself + Imagining the Unimaginable = Revolutions of Our Inner Reality —> Positive Shifts in Our Outer Reality.

"Our power to maximize our potential is based on two important things: (1) the length of our lever—how much potential power and possibility we believe we have, and (2) the position of our fulcrum — the mindset with which we generate the power to change." ~ Achor

Our minds are pre-programmed to behave in certain ways, so they are easily influenced for good or for ill. In one experiment, researchers had different participants play two games: the Wall Street Game and the Community Game. In actuality, both games were one and the same. Nevertheless, this simple name changed how participants chose to play. "The Wall Street Game" made participants more selfish and competitive. "The Community Game " turned players into cooperators. This experiment proves, again, how easy it is to manipulate people. It also highlights the importance of using the right language in social discourse. When you use words of division, you proliferate us vs. them memes and get all the nonsense taking place in our current political climate. But if you use happy and cooperative words, then you create a ripple effect of unknowable, but profound, consequences. By conscious choice, you change the world around you.

Similarly, how you choose to see your work has the same dramatic effect on behavior. Choosing to see your work as a calling enhances engagement, pleasure, and meaning. Choosing to see it as a money-making venture detracts from this sense of purpose. Instead of acting in the interests of the whole, you go "wall-street" mode and become a blight on civilization instead of a light. Our brains are finite machines, capable of focusing on only one or two thought currents at a time. One positive idea connects to other ideas in an associative domino effect. It is not natural for us to hold on to two competing conceptions of ourselves at the same time. Moreover, it is quite difficult to act out those competing conceptions at the same time. When I go competitive mode, I can get pretty mean, and it takes conscious effort to rein in my competitive behavior. The same goes for my moments of selfless altruism. Sometimes, I so thoughtlessly give everything I have to others that it takes effort to stop and consider if they're using me.

It is best to balance optimism with realism, altruism with self-interest. Nevertheless, if you want to lean in one direction, that should be the happy direction. When we look for the good in life, for kindness and excellence and love in the world, our brain must naturally give up looking for the negative. Only so much information can be processed, and the conscious human controls the kind of information that her brain selects for. This screening process results in the "self-fulfilling prophecy". When we accept a belief, we act in ways that make it come true. In one famous experiment, teachers were lied to and told that certain kids were super smart when in fact they were of average intelligence. Nevertheless, this simple lie turned into the truth as the teachers gave these "star" students more help and encouragement throughout the year. By the end, the regular pupils had grown to conform to the expectations of the authority figures around them.

Your beliefs, and the mindset, motivation, and energy you infuse into them, are the determining factors of success in this world. I'll end the section with some simple questions for becoming awesomeness itself. What is the most amazing and best future that I can have during the next three years? What goals do I need to accomplish to get there? What kind of person do I need to become to get there? What are the obstacles? When embarking on this quest for awesomeness, always remind yourself of the reasons you are capable of succeeding. And if you can't come up with the reasons, go out and make them.

Patterns of Reality

Principle # 3 – The Tetris Effect: "When our brains get stuck in a pattern that focuses on stress, negativity, and failure, we set ourselves up to fail. This principle teaches us how to retrain our brains to spot patterns of possibility, so we can see—and seize—opportunity wherever we look."

Our external reality is determined by the content and structure of our thoughts, and by the nature and being of our thoughtlessness. The name, Tetris Effect, comes from an experiment performed by the Harvard Medical School in which researchers paid people to play Tetris for hours. Now, you might think that three days won't change much in the brain, but the participants reported dreaming about Tetris shapes falling from the sky, or they would see shapes in their waking hours, perhaps between two buildings that would be a perfect fit for a Tetris block. Those who have played their fair share of video games (like me) will report the same thing.

Again, this Tetris revolution happened in three days, which shows how quickly we are designed to adapt. Novel activities create neural connections that strengthen and grow with each hour of play. These neural pathways, in turn, literally transform how we perceive the world. And remember, this is just a game of Tetris. Our brains mess with us much more when it comes to the motivations we hold dearly.

Here, let me show you the power of motivated perception. This probably won't work, but, before we start, I want you to make a firm commitment. If you see a farm animal on the next page, then you have to (a) eat a booger or (b) run a mile really fast. But if you see a sea creature on the next page, you get to (a) take the rest of the day off or (b) buy something really nice for yourself. Okay guys, ready? Turn the page! Quick!

So what did you see? Since you were reading about unconscious perceptions, and because I suck at motivating people one way or the other, I doubt that the experiment worked for you. But when psychologist, David Dunning, showed people the picture under test conditions, about 70 percent of them saw what they wanted to see. If the horse picture was primed with positive consequences, more people saw the horse. If the seal picture was tied to one's self interest, then more people saw the seal. This is just how the unconscious mind works. Once we become adults, these preferences for seeing the world a certain way burn them-selves into our neural wiring. While new habits can be learned with greater ease, it is hard to change ingrained habits, and this is especially true when it comes to how we look at the world.

Even though negativity has been shown to undercut our creativity, motivation, and ability to succeed, there are good evolutionary reasons for it. Survival is made easier when you're in fight or flight mode. But while fight or flight is helpful when you have to fight a mastodon, it narrows our focus. We shut down. We stop thinking about we and focus instead on me. We worry about the problem instead of finding a solution. This is how most folks function in our modern day world. They think and behave as if they are in some struggle for survival when, in fact, they're just late for work.

But there is hope! Remember, our brains are flexible. After a few months of deliberate practice, I can personally guarantee you that training the brain to see the good in life leads to more happiness, health, and success. Called the Broaden and Build Theory by Barbara Fredrickson, scientific research has shown that positive emotions make us more creative and open. In one experiment, when participants were primed to feel either anger or amusement, those primed with amusement were able to think bigger and wider thoughts than the angry people. Things like optimism and openness allow us to see opportunities for growth and chase those opportunities with energy. Optimists dig in. They set high goals and they work at them until they succeed. This is science talking, not just me. And science also has specific prescriptions for creating optimism and happiness inside the brain.

(1) Write happiness. Write about what you love.
(2) Journal about hardship and how to move beyond it.
(3) Get into Creativity Training.

With time, we can train our brains to notice the positive patterns of reality over the negative, and I feel like creativity is a huge part of this process. Being creative helps us break out of mental ruts and negative rumination. It is also essential for success in life. Sometimes, when I'm bored or sad, I just start thinking about fun and interesting things. Or I do some lateral thinking puzzles. Here is one for fun. The key is not to get the "right" answer, but to generate as many divergent and novel solutions to the puzzle as possible. The "right" answer is on the next page.

One man is standing on the Taj Mahal. Another guy is on the Eiffel Tower. They both shoot each other, but neither is injured. How is this possible?

Principle # 4 – Falling Up: "In the midst of defeat, stress, and crisis, our brains map different paths to help us cope. This principle is about finding the mental path that not only leads us up out of failure or suffering, but teaches us to be happier and more successful because of it."

Do you know why achieving your goals doesn't make you happy for long? Because of hedonic adaptation. Humans possess natural set points of happiness. No matter how mind-blowing an experience, we get used to it after a while. Studies following paraplegics and lottery winners show that they adapt to previous levels of happiness about a year after their misfortune or windfall. Getting used to happy things sucks and there are ways to prevent that. But it's definitely a good thing to be able to bounce back from negative events. That's what this section is about: how to find resilience in the face of challenges, how to adapt to changing circumstances, and how to overcome difficult obstacles.

Answer: Satellite Photography

Many studies highlight the power of the human spirit by examining a process called post-traumatic growth. So what is PTG? It isn't simply hedonic adaptation. It isn't about individuals getting used to some terrible life event. It isn't about the ability to get over things and move on. Posttraumatic growth is the process by which individuals become better, happier, and more awesome precisely because they had to go through horrible things such as cancer, heart attack, combat, physical assault, and war. Incredibly, people come out of these events with greater love, forgiveness, and gratitude for life. Why? Because they were able to re-frame their adversities. They reinterpreted their existence. Spun it into a positive.

If you look at the lives of some of the most successful people in the world, you will almost certainly find a greater incidence of failure than average. Why? Because they dream of things and try things that no one else is crazy enough to try. Pain is not a bad thing to them. Pain is a good thing. Failure is a learning moment, "a stepping stone to greatness". The Japanese talk about two ways that human beings can grow: kensho and satori. Pain or insight. Of course, we all want to grow the happy way, quickly through moments of satori. But sometimes growth is slow and painful. Sometimes, we need to get knocked on our ass to get our butts in gear.

For many, failure is so important that they look for it in a CEO. And more important than failure, they like to see people who bounce back and overcome their obstacles. This ability to overcome, to master your life and feel that you have power and control over it, is called self-efficacy. Read Arnold Toynbee. Crises and challenges are what drive human civilization. We wouldn't have created empires and technology if the world was a cake walk. The challenge of nature is what humans are meant to master, both mother nature and human nature. Regarding human nature, crises are often the genesis of creative growth for the individual.

So, my purpose right now is to give you the mental toolkit to help you creatively overcome your challenges. The first structure of thought is given to us by the Buddha. This is the ideal structure, involving a process by which we directly confront the problem. Most people follow Buddhist teachings because they like meditation or the values of Buddhism. Few, however, recognize the logical brilliance of Siddharta Gautama. Just take a look at his Four Noble Truths. Here they are in their original form.

>Buddha's Four Noble Truths.
>(1) There is suffering.
>(2) There is an origin and cause of suffering, which is egoic desire, delusion, ignorance, and anger.
>(3) There is a way to stop suffering, which is nirvana and the cessation of desire.
>(4) There is an eightfold path to nirvana, and this path ultimately leads to the other shore.

Of course, the Buddha, in all of his wisdom, speaks of the most fundamental problem of human nature, dukkha (suffering). But let's put that aside and look at the linked logic of the Four Truths, which can be applied to any specific situation. Here they are in pure structure.

Structure of the Noble Truths
(1) There is problem A.
(2) There is a cause B for problem A.
(3) The solution to A is the negation of B.
(4) The treatment C solves A by negating B.

Or if the solution is not to be found, there is the second structure of thinking called the ABCD model of interpretation, which involves simply changing your beliefs about the event that you cannot change. Scientists have found that the happiest people explain their life stories in positive ways. They see things with just a bit of shine, and this shine is crucial to successful living.

The ABCD structure allows you to create an optimistic explanatory style of reality. Remember, you should really burn this style of thought into your brain. That way, it comes naturally. So, here it is:

(1) Adversity — the event that we cannot change.
(2) Belief — our reaction to the event.
(3) Consequence — the mental paths that your mind takes as a result of your interpretation of the event.
(4) Disputation — if those mental paths are negative, then you need to, first, find the crappy belief, and then challenge it to change your interpretation.

43

Circles Within Circles

Principle # 5 – "The Zorro Circle: When challenges loom and we get overwhelmed, our rational brains can get hijacked by emotions. This principle teaches us how to regain control by focusing first on small, manageable goals, and then gradually expanding our circle to achieve bigger and bigger ones."

Self-efficacy is about possessing the feeling of mastery over one's life. But sometimes things can get so hectic that you don't know which way is up. When actions never produce the results that you intend, you get this feeling of helplessness. This feeling, if it isn't taken care of, will totally ruin and control your life. It will make you super depressed if continuously indulged in. I'm sure that you guys remember the dog experiments about learned helplessness. Here's a summary. In one experiment, psychologists shocked the dogs at regular intervals, which I think is pretty mean. The dogs had no way to stop the pain. No matter what they did, the shock would come at regular intervals. Then, when the dogs were placed in another experiment, in an environment where they could easily stop the shocks from happening, they failed to do so. Why? Because they learned to be helpless. They transferred failure from one domain of life to another domain.

One crucial element, one foundational pillar, of success is the knowledge that your behaviors make a difference, that we have control over our fate, that what I do now will change my future for the better. How do we gain confidence in our self-efficacy? In what can only be called a stroke of brilliance because he references Zorro, Shawn Achor talks about how people consciously make progress towards their goals by focusing on the mini-rituals.

When our lives get out of control, even doing the daily rituals seems to be too much work. For example, if you have tons of homework and you don't want to get started, then you have to set a mini-goal. Okay. For the next ten minutes, I will focus on the easiest and funnest part of the work. After that is done, I will take a little break, and then I will tackle this next part of the work, and so on and so forth. Take on small challenges. When they are met, you feel like, "Yes, I'm making progress. I'm going somewhere." And that is what gives you the little bursts of happiness leading to a greater sense of control. It's the best way to engage in habit formation. If you want to create new daily rituals, start small and build from there. This practice, known as kaizen in Japanese, comes from the principle that small positive steps are what make a person's journey. Feelings of mastery are proven to improve work performance. You work harder. You work smarter. And you work happier.

Once you master the small challenges, you'll be surprised at how quickly you expand your circle and totally upgrade your daily rituals. In turn, this upgrade radically increases the chances you'll achieve your life goals. And when you reach your goals, you move towards your purpose. And when you move towards your purpose, you're helping everyone out, not just yourself.

44
Time and Energy

Principle # 6 – "The 20-Second Rule: Sustaining lasting change often feels impossible because our willpower is limited. And when willpower fails, we fall back on our old habits and succumb to the path of least resistance. This principle shows how, by making small energy adjustments, we can reroute the path of least resistance and replace bad habits with good ones."

"We are what we repeatedly do.
Excellence, then, is not an act, but a habit."
~ Aristotle

Simple exercise in formal logic. $A(x) \longrightarrow H(x)$. Now, x is time and energy. A is every single action that you habitually engage in. What do you do when you wake up? What about when you're on the toilet? Does your thinking change during the day? x is not a constant, but a variable producing different results depending on context. x is not a simple behavior. It can be a complex set of behaviors leading to positive or negative outcomes. Now, the question is: what determines whether something is positive or negative? Another quote for you:

"Happiness, not gold or prestige, is the ultimate currency of life."
~ Tal Ben Shahar

For the materially minded people, try to think about happiness as a unit of good. H is the amount of happiness that results from each tiny action. You want to maximize happiness by investing your limited x in ways that yield the most and highest quality H. Seriously pursue this analysis. Apply this knowledge to your life. Once you have an idea of what results in happiness and what doesn't, make a conscious effort to change those habits that yield no happiness, and craft those habits that do. The goal here is to set mini and maxi habits that automatically pay off in life satisfaction without your having to struggle to maintain them. William James famously said, "All our life, so far as it has definite form, is but a mass of habits."

Now, the question is: What is a habit? Charles Duhrigg in his fantastic book, The Power of Habit, defines it thusly: "the choices that all of us deliberately make at some point, and then stop thinking about but continue doing, often every day." Habits are loops of behavior consisting of three elements. Cue: the stimulus that starts the neural mechanism of behavior. Routine: the unconscious carrying out of said habit through thought and action. Reward: the psychological satisfaction, that hit of happiness, you feel from completing said action. It's a circle because each action only burns the habit deeper into our brains.

cue → routine → reward — "habit loop"

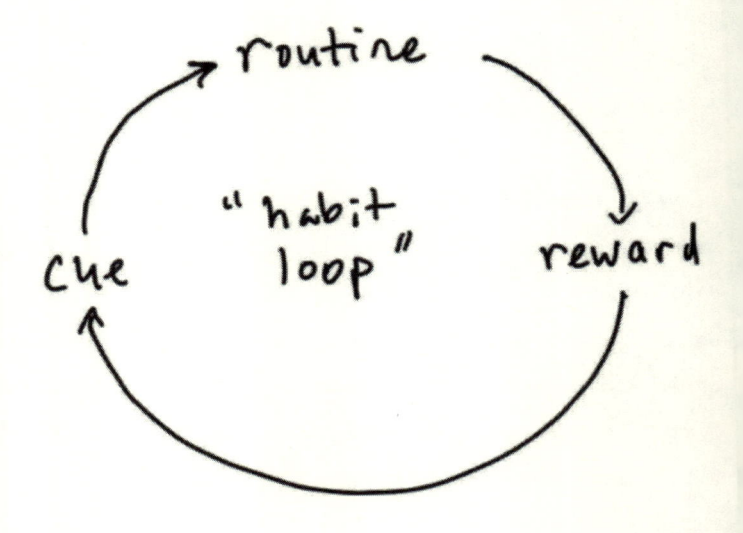

Here's the picture again. X is the cue. A is the routine. H is the reward. This is the structure of thought that you can use to apply to the content of your life. Filter all of your habits through this thought equation. But knowing this picture isn't enough. You have to know it, apply it, and then do it.

Everyone knows that the doing is the hard part. But if we're clever about it, we can hack these habits and make them easier to bend to our will. Duhrigg talks about replacing the routine of bad habits, the A, with other healthier routines. Say you want to stop smoking pot. The presence of weed is the cue. You do it because the high is a reward in itself. The routine of actually getting high is the thing that needs to change. One good routine is to go for a run. Another is to meditate. Another is to think happy thoughts. Good routines are anything that give you the reward of psychological satisfaction without actually smoking weed. Change the routine. And when you change the routine, clearly define a cue, like choosing the same time each day to go for a run, and then make sure to reward yourself at the end. It's as simple as that.

But simple isn't easy. How does one best change the routine? Shawn Achor does it by plugging another step into the circle. The 20 Second Rule. You can use this rule to nudge every part of the habit loop in one direction or another. Basically, by making bad habits twenty seconds more difficult to indulge in, and good habits twenty seconds easier, you quintuple the chances of breaking or making the habit.

If the path to success is the process of making good habits automatic, the only way to do that is to manipulate the dynamics of time and energy around you. When doing good becomes effortless, then you know that you're on the right track. You may not be successful in material terms, but that's not what awesomeness is. Awesomeness is the inside job. It's about investing in brain habits that naturally pay off in happiness dividends. You are putting happiness units in the bank for future withdrawal. And remember, happiness is the end to which we ought to aim all our efforts, not money or power.

In his entertainingly eclectic book, The Happiness Equation, Neil Parsicha shows us how most people go about creating new habits.

Can Do ⟶ Want To Do ⟶ Do

But we all know that you don't just suddenly become good at meditating or writing books. Usually, can do is the last thing you're actually able to do, and this is why we never end up running marathons or becoming Buddhas or famous authors. But there's another way to go about habit formation.

Do ⟶ Can Do ⟶ Want To Do

Often, if we just start doing, our brains (1) learn to enjoy the new habit, (2) learn to execute the habit effectively, and (3) learn to engage in the habit effortlessly.

"A tendency to act only becomes effectively ingrained in us in proportion to the uninterrupted frequency with which the actions actually occur, the brain grows to their use. In other words, habits form because our brain actually changes in response to frequent practice."
-William James.

Remember neuroplasticity. Our brains are like roads that get stronger the more often we drive over them. Our neural pathways bend, break, and reconnect in infinite ways. Think about those spaghetti junctions in cities with many high roads over one area. Now multiply that by a billion and imagine that it's a living organism. That's what your brain is like. Those roads solidify with age, practice, and habit. Sometimes, they get so stable that traffic naturally runs along them without god (that's us) coming in and consciously willing something to happen.

>(1) It takes about 21 days to create stable habits. When you make commitments to yourself, remember this number.

>(2) Inactivity is the easiest habit to fall into. The more we do it, the more it happens. The funny part is: we don't like it as much as we think we do. Studies prove that passive habits, if indulged for more than 30 minutes at a stretch, result in what psychologists call psychic entropy.

>(3) Fortunately, active leisure hobbies like running engage parts of the brain that people describe as true happiness. Unfortunately, active leisure hobbies, like chemical reactions, require greater activation energy to get things going. Good habits are often, by their very nature, energy and time intensive. But once you get over this hurdle, then everything becomes automatic and your good habits lead you through life in a happy and healthy way.

4. How do you pick the right habits? Check the happiness meter inside your brain called self awareness. Once you know what makes you happy, you have to break down the habit loop and tinker with the mini-behaviors within each behavior. Use the routine replacement tactic.

Below is the rest of the section summarized and simplified. The Foundational Habits Necessary for Habit Change Zorro Circle <> 20 Second Rule <> Social Support <> Purposeful Life (Growth Goals) <> Meditation<> Creatively Thinking About How You Can Change <> Consistently Regulating Your Behavior <> Consistent Standards <> Being Happy = Effective Habit Transformation

45
Good Friends, Awesome Life

Principle # 7 – "Social Investment: In the midst of challenges and stress, some people choose to hunker down and retreat within themselves. But successful people invest in their friends, peers, and family members to propel themselves forward. This principle teaches us how to invest more in one of the greatest predictors of success and excellence — our social support network."

One of the goals of science is to attempt to understand the complex relations of reality by isolating two or three variables and studying them. When it comes to happiness, there are so many processes, psychological and social, that it's usually hard to know exactly what makes people happy. Usually. One thing is certain about the happiness formula, and it's that our social relationships impact our happiness more than any other factor. One study, called the Harvard Men study, followed 268 men for 70 years. After looking at decades of data and dozens of factors that might contribute to happiness, psychologists came to one simple conclusion: Love, connection to others, was the one factor that separated those with the happiest lives from those who were unhappy.

Now of course, being happy, healthy, and surrounded by quality human beings that motivate and inspire you, all lead to greater career achievement, wealth and, if you're that kind of monkey, social status in the corporate hierarchy. Now, the question is: Exactly how do social relationships make us more likely to succeed? There is the happiness part, of course. But is there a direct link?

Quality Friends <—> Job Performance

Definitely. Think about it. When you have good friends and a good boss, you want to produce quality work simply because you want them not to hate you. Moreover, we already know how much our environment determines behavior. One study found that 20 minutes outside in sunny weather creates positive emotions, which also enhances working memory and creativity. If this is what the weather does, imagine what a good or bad boss can do to your brain power. Compared to intrinsic and social forms of motivation, studies have shown that money is often counterproductive when it comes to complex and creative tasks. More important than money is cultivating a bond with your colleagues; a common sense of purpose in whatever field you're involved in. Let's look at some of the techniques that Shawn gives us for maximizing relationships. (1) Eye contact triggers empathy and rapport. (2) Asking interesting questions about the other person. (3) Initiating conversations that are not task oriented. (4) Meeting with people face to face.

This also applies to the ideas of Shelly Gable, a psychologist at the University of California. She has found that how you react to another person's good news is often more important for nourishing relationships than how you react to bad news. There are, apparently, four ways you can respond. The best way you can do it is the active and constructive response. This is when you're enthusiastic and follow up the good news with specific comments and questions.

"Gable's studies have shown that active-constructive responding enhances relationship commitment and satisfaction and fuels the degree to which people feel understood, validated, and cared for during a discussion" ~ Shawn Achor

Bending Time

In one brilliantly simple insight, Neil Parischa gives us the basic math for structuring our lives. If you think about it, each week has 168 hours in it (7x 24), which divides perfectly into three baskets of 56 hours each. Coincidentally, most peoples' lives fall into three baskets as well. Here's a picture.

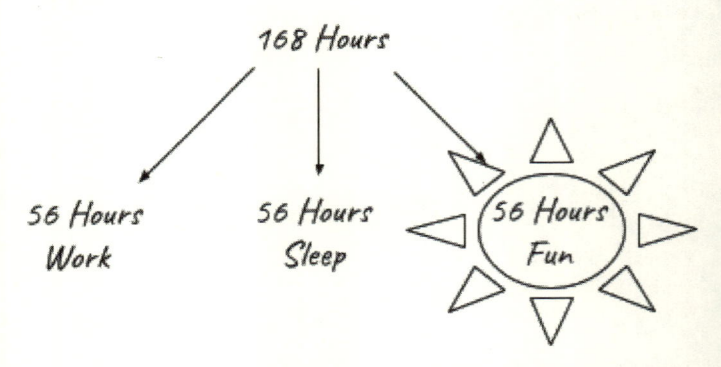

168 Hours → 56 Hours Work / 56 Hours Sleep / 56 Hours Fun

Most people sleep about 8 hours a night, and they work about 8 hours a day. Now, give and take a few hours of sleep and work, you get about 56 hours a week to do what you want and love to do. Why is this important? (1) By consciously structuring your life, you know how best to move time from one bucket to another. (2) By looking at life this way, you can consider the interactions between the buckets.

The permutations are endless, but the point is this: Time is the ultimate finite resource. Every second you spend is a second you'll never get back. Think about that, and then think about all the time you waste not optimizing personal happiness or pursuing meaningful goals.

Science tells us that effective time management minimizes stress, depression, and academic failure. But the issue is deeper than that. If you live until the age of 80, your heart beats 3.4 billion times before the end. That's 100,000 times a day. It is a set amount. Finite. Limited. Do you want to spend millions of heartbeats on things that make you sad and useless or awesome and happy? It's your choice.

I'll finish this section by trying a third time to catalyze an existential hole of dread in your soul. Observe what's called the Cantril Self-Anchoring Striving Scale. It connects our values, life goals, and ideal life to where we stand right now. And I quote Daniel Kahneman's book, Thinking Fast and Slow:

Please imagine a ladder with steps numbered from zero at the bottom to 10 at the top. The top of the ladder represents the best possible life for you and the bottom of the ladder represents the worst possible life for you. On which step of the ladder would you say you personally feel you stand at this time?

The Habit of Happiness

So far, we've discussed what makes us happy. We have touched on the why a little. Now, we focus on the process of actually getting happy. In The How of Happiness, the researcher, Sonja Lyubomirsky, details twelve science back strategies for making a happier you.

$$\text{Happiness Formula}$$
$$H = S + C + V$$
$$H = \text{level of happiness}$$
$$S = \text{biological set point (50\%)}$$
$$C = \text{outer conditions of your life (10\%)}$$
$$V = \text{intentional activities (40\%)}$$

Most people believe happiness is something that you must passively accept. This is partially true. Your parent's genes account for about 50% of your well being. Other people in our materialistic culture say, "It's money, baby. It's all about power and sex." But there are many forms of power, young padawan. Yes, there is what I call monkey power, which accounts for about 10% of your happiness. But there is also this thing called soul power, driven by intention and introspection, which is the ability to look inside your head and take control of your thought patterns.

Neuroplasticity tells us that what fires together, wires together. Thinking happy thoughts strengthens your neural pathways of happiness, optimism, and motivation by infusing associative networks of positivity into your brain. The more this happens, the happier you get. On an unconscious level, one happy idea connects to hundreds of others in a cascade effect of joy and love, creating an upwards spiral of awesomeness that radically transforms your life.

Ultimately, we wire our brains into happiness generators by cultivating self-awareness. You need to be aware of what you do and what you think (and don't do and don't think), and how and why those actions (or inactions) lead to your happiness or unhappiness. Just follow your mood for a day. And then connect your emotions to what you're doing. Once you become aware of your daily habits and moods, then you can better appreciate the power of the upcoming happiness interventions. Everybody is slightly different, so try them all and see what works for you.

1. Express Gratitude
2. Cultivate Optimism
3. Avoid Overthinking and Social Comparisons
4. Practice Acts of Kindness
5. Nurture Your Relationships
6. Develop Coping Strategies During Times of Depression
7. Learn to Forgive

8. Increase Flow Experiences

9. Enjoy the Little Things (and Really Enjoy the Big Things)

10. Set Goals

11. Spirituality and Meditation

- And I quote the author: "An avalanche of studies has shown that meditation has multiple positive effects on a person's happiness and positive emotions, on physiology, stress, cognitive abilities, and physical health, as well as other harder to assess attributes, like "self-actualization" and "moral maturity".

12. Exercise

The Science of Exercise

There are many benefits of exercise. It strengthens our hearts, bones, and muscles. It teaches us self-discipline and reduces our risk for disease. It improves the quality of your sleep. It does all kinds of things, but the focus of this section is the influence of exercise on mental health. The following benefits stem from scientific research on the relationship between the body and the brain.

(1) In cases of mild to moderate depression or anxiety, studies have shown that exercise is as effective as medication.

(2) Exercise creates BDNF, or brain derived neurotrophic growth factor, which stimulates neurogenesis; the production of brain cells. BDNF is popularly called miracle grow for the brain.

The Science of Meditation

Meditation is perhaps the most effective tool you have against the slings and arrows of fate. You cannot control the world, but you can control your reaction to the world. Meditation does many things to the mind and body. (1) It anchors you in the present moment by helping you go beyond thought. This in turn reduces anxiety and regret because thought occurs in time, and you need the future to be anxious and you need the past to be regretful. (2) Meditation puts space between you and your thoughts, giving you control over the contents of consciousness. (3) Meditation reduces activity in the default mode network (the me me me network), and this produces actual changes in the brain, promoting qualities such as empathy and compassion. (4) Evidence has shown that meditation can increase the enzyme telomerase, which is responsible for building telomeres, or cancer reducing molecules, in the body. (5) The act of regular meditation improves cognitive function, reduces stress, increases emotional regulation, and boosts memory. This was found by Harvard researchers who discovered increases in gray matter in key areas of the brain. Overall, meditation can change your life if you put in the time and effort.

50
Connecting the Dots

In order to live a life of awesomeness, you have to ground it in certain first principles and basic facts about reality. Just take a look at the world around you. The skyscrapers, computers, solar panels, books, aquariums; all of them are there because of science. You can't have supercomputers and the internet without quantum mechanics. You can't have surgery and medicine without the brilliance of doctors and engineers. No matter what your particular set of beliefs, you have to give it to science for creating much of the goodness we see in the world today. Moreover, you have to put stock in the academic institutions and the mavens doing the science in the first place. They're not only smart people; a good many of them do what they do out of a sense of purpose and moral obligation to humanity.

But the people making up academia are ephemeral. They all come and go in the pursuit of truth. It's the theories, the truth, that interests the real seekers. And here's one enormous truth that everyone has to believe in for the sake of humanity's continued existence: evolution. If you don't believe in evolution, your worldview depends on religious thoughts written by men who lived during the dark ages; times of brutal violence and tribalism. Evolution determines so much of how we see the world. It's so foundational that political, religious, and social thinking are impoverished without it.

Once you look at religion, you find major contradictions in every holy text. One second it's all kumbaya peace and love hippie stuff, and the next you have God demanding sacrifice and the no holds barred extermination of enemy tribes. It is as if God is bipolar or something. And yet, it all becomes clear if you look at life through an evolutionary lens. As a social institution, religion is designed to promote in-group harmony and out-group aggression. It's built on our most primal instincts; the desire for survival and proliferation. Since natural selection takes place more on the tribal level than the individual, any ideology that promotes group fitness is going to thrive in the brutal world of yesteryear. Religion doesn't get rid of Darwinian natural selection. It just pushes it up to the group level. And I quote Micheal Shermer in his excellent book, The Science of Good and Evil:

"Because our deep moral sentiments evolved as part of our behavioral repertoire of responses for survival in a complex social environment, we carry the seeds of such in-group inclusiveness today. Israeli psychologist Georges Tamarin tested this hypothesis in 1966 on 1,066 schoolchildren ages eight to fourteen, by presenting them with the story of the battle of Jericho in Josh 6. Joshua told his people to rejoice because God granted them access to Jericho; "Then they utterly destroyed all in the city, both men and women, young and old, oxen, sheep, and asses, with the edge of the sword....

Tamarin wanted to test how biblical stories influenced children, particularly those stories that touted the superiority of monotheism, focused on the notion of the "chosen people," and made acts of genocide heroic. After presenting the Joshua story, the children were asked: Do you think Joshua and the Israelites acted rightly or not? Tamarin offered them three answers from which to choose: A, approval; B, partial approval or disapproval; and C, total disapproval. The results were disturbing: 66 percent of the children completely approved of the Israelites' murderous actions, while only 8 percent chose B and 26 percent chose C."

In a brilliant addition, Tamarin proved that such religious beliefs pervert common sense moral reasoning. Shermer continues:

"Substituting "General Lin" for Joshua and a "Chinese Kingdom 3,000 years ago" for Israel, Tamarin found that only 7 percent of his Israeli subjects (a control group of 168 different children) approved of the genocide, while a full 75 percent disapproved totally...Between group competition (with other hominid and primate groups) for limited resources led to the selection for such immoral sentiments as competitiveness and selfishness, but at the same time it led to within group cooperation and selflessness that enhanced the fitness level of individual members of the group."

It's the belief, the belief in the infallibility of religion, that messed with these kids' heads, that robbed them of their moral faculties. Otherwise, they are just fine. If nothing else, the Nazis were meticulous record keepers. One document details religious affiliations of the general population in the years leading up to the Holocaust: 54% self identified as Protestants, 40% identified as Catholics, 3.5% as deist, and 1.5% as atheist. Just look at the movies we watch even today. They're mostly filled with blood, gore, sex, money, and power. Why does Hollywood love this stuff? It's because violence and sex sell. They tap our most primal drives. Simple as that.

Religion emerged as an aid to survival in order to express, refine, and exploit our baser impulses. It's the power of the lower brain. It's the reason that our happiness set point and our emotions are largely determined by genetics. Emotions are evolutionary modules functioning to influence our ethical judgments and, in turn, the power relations between members within or between groups. Emotions are intelligent in their own way. They are surges of feeling, changing our interpretation of reality, in order to help us deal with the threats and opportunities faced by our ancestors millions of years ago.

Basic List of Emotions

(1) Guilt and Shame: A feeling that changes our behavior because we have not conformed to the social rules of our tribe. When

rules are just, this is a good thing. When they're unjust, conformity and obedience ruins nations and kills innocents.

(2) Anger: survival based energy aimed at righting perceived wrongs or defeating an enemy that refuses to respect your ideals or property. Humans have spent 99% of their existence as hunters and competitors. Winning is in our nature, and anger (mixed with a heavy cudgel) used to help us get our way in terms of survival and resources.

(3) Sympathy and Gratitude: promotes bonding, the sharing of resources, and increases the probability of cooperation and forming alliances with other individuals or groups.

(4) Joy: promotes bonding through shared emotions and, eventually, values. It opens us up to the other. Laughter is the quickest link between two individuals. Science shows that we recognize happy faces more quickly than sad or angry faces. When someone smiles, you can't help but smile, even if you try to control it.

(5) Fear and Disgust: survival instinct that helps us avoid things, individuals, or groups that are potential threats. It's often wedded to moral judgments and has been used to justify the most terrible atrocities in history.

(6) Surprise: startle response to an unexpected event.

(7) Elevation, the emotion of awesomeness: We'll talk about this one a lot in a second, but it's usually described as awe and reverence for something greater than the egoic self. It turns off the "I" and elicits altruism and virtuous behavior. But this emotion is also misused, since it promotes the survival of one's genes by pushing the human ape to risk his life for his tribe. I'm sure that it was a moment of elevation that inspired most of the preachers in our world today. They felt "called" when it was actually their neurochemistry acting up. Unless counteracted with autonomous moral thought, the repeated experience of elevation with the same small group of individuals allows spiritual leaders to brainwash, control, and abuse their followers. Or it gives people this sense of cosmic mission. "My God is only one that can make a person feel so good and so loving. Thus, it's my moral duty to convert the heathens, those of lesser faiths."

Moral Foundations of Human Society

Each of these emotions is connected to certain physiological responses, forcing the body to release hormones or alter heart-rate in order to create the neural conditions necessary for the experience of happiness or anger. More importantly, each of these emotions has social implications, forming the essence of the moral foundations of human society. Mark Matousek summarizes the five basic moral dimensions of human civilization below. These dimensions are universal across times and cultures; from the loving unity of the Kung bushmen of Africa to the heart of darkness found in Nazi Germany.

(1) First, we're concerned with harm and care. As "communitarians under the skin" who survive through interconnection, and disliked seeing or feeling the pain of others, we have especially keen moral emotions related to threat as well as nurturing. This foundation underlies kindness and all forms of emotions and physical succor and protection.

(2) Second, we're devoted to justice and fairness, the rules of reciprocity, autonomy, reputation management, revenge, and punishment that enable us to live as individuals in groups. This foundation generates laws and rights and depends on an underlying, unavoidable, sometimes self centered belief in just deserts.

(3) Third, we depend on in-group loyalty for our survival. This foundation engenders patriotism, tribal pride, and self-sacrifice for the community; it's also why we automatically treat out-group members differently than our personal cohorts, and always worse. Loyalty is crucial to ethics, but in-group favoritism is also our nemesis as it underlies tribal conflict, war, and aggression.

(4) Fourth, we care about authority and respect. As hierarchical animals with pecking orders to consider, we have a strong,

instinctive attraction towards leadership and respect of elders, as well as reverence for tradition. This foundation is both an enormous help, as when good authority figures lead us to higher ground, and a moral hazard, as when power mongers dupe us with charisma or we allow ourselves to forgo ethics in favor of obedience to questionable people or causes.

(5) Fifth, we have an innate elevating need for purity and sacredness. This foundation, rooted in our central moral emotion, disgust, turns us from animality toward the divine. This hunger for purity can be abused when an individual or nation or faith flays on our disgust reflex by portraying enemies as morally impure, as in the case of anti-Semites and homophobes.

These basic moral dimensions influence each other to produce the cultural diversity we see in the world today. When in-group loyalty combines with authority and a tradition of nationalism, you get Nazi Germany. When elevation merges with ideals of care and fairness, you get the Dalai Lama. And such emotions, or ways of being, are contagious. Memes are the ideological layer upon these basic emotions. They travel through populations like the wind, leading to everything from concentration camps to non-violent moral revolutions. Our brains are wired to connect and merge with others, and the mechanism for this connection is the "mirror neuron".

The Neurochemistry of Loving Oneness

The average neuron has about ten thousand connections to its neighbors. These cells form, break, and reform in near infinite variety. Whatever you believe consciousness is, you cannot deny that its functioning is inextricably bound to the physical brain. Everything we are, our thoughts, emotions, perceptions, intelligence, personality, and our sense of self, is determined by this two pound ball of slush pulsating between our ears. The smallest shifts in the structure or chemistry of the brain can result in enormous swings in who "you" are. Before and during much of my hippie phase, I was a determined atheist. After my first spiritual experience (which incidentally took place before I ever touched psychedelics), everything changed in an instant.

What happened in my brain to cause this experience? I don't know. But the feeling itself was the happiest happy, the highest ecstasy, the experience of this visual archetype that spun and spun in a circle, spiraling into the center until it culminated in a moment of complete self-transcendent bliss and loss of personhood.

Did some neurochemical shift cause the process? Who knows. Afterwards, what followed was much spiritual discipline, unnecessary pain, and self-denial culminating in my first LSD experience, which blasted me out of my body and into a higher state of consciousness; later eliciting a psychotic episode that took me three years of suffering to completely get over. The eventual return to sanity came with the higher state of consciousness necessary to maintain it. These days, I'm in my body only when I'm not paying attention. The second I focus my prefrontal cortex, I become everything and nothing. "Anshu" doesn't exist as he once did. With effort and by thinking about things, I can bring him back, but otherwise who I am is anybody's guess. But one thing is undeniable. It's certainly a higher state of consciousness. I'm more happy, conscious, creative, empathetic, and funny than I ever was before the experience. I have near complete control of my thoughts. I can shut them off whenever I want to.

Anyways, I wanted to tell that story to illustrate the power of the tiniest neuro-chemical changes in the brain, and how they can change the course of your life. LSD is dangerous. I wouldn't recommend it unless you absolutely insist on taking tremendous risks. But for most people, LSD is a one or two time experience, so imagine what regular emotions do to your brain and body in comparison. Anger regularly washes the body in hormones such as adrenaline and cortisol. Fear similarly stimulates your heart rate and the fight-or-flight response. Happiness silences the brain centers connected to negative thought, helping you focus and recover from stress. And finally, there's the emotion of love, a parasympathetic state of calmness, which is the opposite of the fight-or-flight response.

In his book, The Happiness Hypothesis, the psychologist Jonathan Haidt goes into the neurophysiology of love. Often, the feelings commonly associated with love are in fact an entirely different emotion; something he calls elevation. So what is elevation? It's not the feeling of getting high on stuff. Elevation is a unique experience that people have when witnessing acts of moral heroism or altruism. Thomas Jefferson talked about it a long time ago. Haidt, writes, "Jefferson gives us most of the major components: an eliciting or triggering condition (displays of charity, gratitude, or other virtues); physical changes in the body (dilation in the chest); a motivation (a desire of doing charitable and grateful acts also); and a characteristic feeling beyond bodily sensations (elevated sentiments)."

Most people have experienced this emotion. You feel lifted, calm, and all fuzzy inside. It's a highly refined and subtle form of happiness; a brief taste of self-transcendence. The Hindus talk about the subtle body, the heart chakra, and the anandamaya kosha. Elevation is the reason cultures come together around stories of moral leaders such as Lincoln and Gandhi. Through lab experiments, Dr. Haidt and Sara Algoe have isolated the emotion of moral elevation from the other emotions like love, happiness, and nonmoral forms of admiration.

Moreover, other people have done research into the neural correlates of elevation. Apparently, elevation stimulates the vagus nerve and the production of oxytocin. The vagus nerve connects to the heart and lungs, functioning to calm the body. Meanwhile, oxytocin elicits feelings of attachment and bonding, and possibly works with the vagus nerve to create the emotions of gratitude and companionate love. I'd continue writing about this stuff, but Mark Matousek says it better.

"To test the theory of elevation, Haidt and an assistant gathered forty two lactating women together in his lab at the University of Virginia. Half of the nursing mothers watched a poignant episode of Oprah involving a rehabilitated gang member. The remaining group of nursing women spent their time watching an ordinary episode of Seinfeld. The elevation difference between these two groups was dramatic. The Oprah watching moms overwhelmingly leaked milk into their pads (the sign of oxytocin lifting them) and nursed their babies afterward. Hardly any of the Seinfeld watchers so much as wetted a pad. Elevation had made the Oprah mothers more generous and loving."

According to researchers, people with high vagal tone seem to be better at building relationships, dealing with loss, handling stress, and even endurance running. When the vagus nerve activates, it slows our heart rate and breathing down. It plays a big role in the mind-body connection, and so consciously tending to the breath trains the nerve and allows us to access this state of calm whenever we need it. Finally, the experience of elevation might point to the neural correlates of the experience that Hindus have for generations called enlightenment.

Elevating the World

Structuring the choice architecture of society towards inducing states of elevation may just be the best way to save the world. Too often, the emotion is monopolized by religions when it could just as easily be created in secular formats. Look at the basic list of emotions. Each is autonomous, but connected in different ways. More elevation means more happiness and less sadness. More gratitude means more elevation and less anger. Light and darkness exist together in the universe, the yin and the yang, and yet more of one necessarily entails less of the other. Our world is awash in divisions over everything from football teams to national power. The story of genocide in Joshua is nothing special, and it's an impulse all of us have indulged in one way or another. Everybody ties themselves to certain people, groups, and authorities. Everybody follows rules set down by somebody else. That's often a good thing. But in the case of those school kids tested by Tamarin, it most certainly wasn't.

I wonder what those kids would have done if, before the study, Tamarin asked them to emphatically put themselves in the shoes of the women and children of Jericho; if he had primed those kids to look through the eyes of another. It's this capacity that elevating stories nurture. They help us transcend the mundane, petty, and quotidian. Elevation feeds the noble and weakens the ignoble. It breaks down the boundaries of the ego, the little "me", and helps us connect to all of humanity.

Think about what meditation does to the mind. Transcending thought means transcending all of the ideas, behaviors, and memes unique to your particular culture. In the realm of stillness, you enter the realm of humanity. Once you see the human race as one single people, we can work to face the problems threatening our evolving world civilization.

"We must not allow the ignoble to injure the noble, or the smaller to injure the greater. Those who nourish the smaller parts will become small men. Those who nourish the greater parts will become great men." ~ Meng Tzu

Flatland

So far, we've been talking about the vertical dimensions of human society, that of status and hierarchy, and the horizontal dimensions of individuals, in-group members, and out-group neighbors. The prescription of this book has been to flatten hierarchies to the greatest degree possible, maintaining distinctions on the basis of role and merit, while simultaneously expanding our horizontal embrace to encompass all of humanity. In his book, Haidt adds another dimension to the mix, the vertical dimension, and uses an excellent story by Edwin Abbot to illustrate the nature, the essential mystery, of spirituality.

The story is called Flatland, and it takes place in a two dimension world in which all of the inhabitants are squares, circles, and other flat shapes. This world of Flatland operates by a different set of rules than our three dimensional world. Their houses and societies are built according to the limited principles of the two dimensional knowledge, the knowledge of space and lines.

"Windows there are none in our houses; for the light comes to us alike in our homes and out of them, by day and by night, equally at all times and in all places, whence we know not. It was in old days, with our learned men, an interesting and oft-investigated question, "What is the origin of light?" and the solution of it has been repeatedly attempted, with no other result than to crowd our lunatic asylums with the would-be solvers."

Briefly, the hero of our story, a simple square mathematician from Flatland, encounters the monarch from the one dimensional world, Lineland, and tries to explain the concept of borders and space, but in vain. "It seemed that this poor ignorant Monarch – as he called himself – was persuaded that the Straight Line which he called his Kingdom, and in which he passed his existence, constituted the whole of the world, and indeed the whole of Space. His subjects – of whom the small Lines were men and the Points Women – were all alike confined in motion and eyesight to that single Straight Line, which was their World."

Ultimately, the square gives up on the monarch of Lineland, and is soon visited by a Teacher; a sphere from the higher dimension of Spaceland. Initially, the square does not perceive the Teacher to be anything special. He sees the sphere as a circle using his limited two dimensional vision. "I am indeed, in a certain sense a Circle," replied the Voice, "and a more perfect Circle than any in Flatland; but to speak more accurately, I am many Circles in one."

By vein of reason, the sphere tries to explain the principles of the vertical dimension, the dimension of height as well as length and width, but the poor square fails to grasp the point, collapsing the vertical dimension into his ideas of north and south on a map; the only things his senses can perceive.

"Sphere. Why will you refuse to listen to reason? I had hoped to find in you – as being a man of sense and an accomplished mathematician – a fit apostle for the Gospel of the Three Dimensions, which I am allowed to preach once only in a thousand years; but now I know not how to convince you. Stay, I have it. Deeds, and not words, shall proclaim the truth. Listen, my friend."

Through deeds, the Teacher convinces the pupil of his power. The sphere "magically" grows and shrinks from smaller to larger to smaller circles as he uses the third dimension to enter and leave the second dimension. The sphere even disappears from Flatland completely only to reappear at the other end of the squares' house. And since the sphere is on a higher dimension, he can see into everyone's house and every room. He shows the square that he knows who is where and even what is in his cupboard, taking objects out of the cupboard without opening it and producing them to the square. Such feats amaze the square, but fail to adequately convince him. Reason ultimately cannot do the job. Spirituality must be tasted, must be experienced, before it's finally accepted. In frustration, the sphere yanks the square out of Flatland and into the higher dimension of Spaceland.

"An unspeakable horror seized me. There was a darkness; then a dizzy, sickening sensation of sight that was not like seeing; I saw a Line that was no Line; Space that was not Space: I was myself, and not myself. When I could find voice, I shrieked aloud in agony, "Either this is madness or it is Hell." "It is neither," calmly replied the voice of the Sphere, "it is Knowledge; it is Three Dimensions; open your eye once again and try to look steadily."

"I looked, and, behold, a new world!" The square is amazed just as Arjuna was when Krishna displayed his universal form in the Gita.

The Teacher continues. "I am a Being, composed as I told you before, of many Circles, the Many in the One, called in this country a Sphere. And, just as the outside of a Cube is a Square, so the outside of a Sphere presents the appearance of a Circle."

"After this, as we floated gently back to Flatland, I could hear the mild voice of my Companion pointing the moral of my vision, and stimulating me to aspire, and to teach others to aspire. He had been angered at first – he confessed – by my ambition to soar to Dimensions above the Third; but, since then, he had received fresh insight, and he was not too proud to acknowledge his error to a Pupil."

The square attempts to convert his fellows in Flatland, but in vain. They are too entranced by the shadows, by the world they see with their senses and not the world that can only be perceived with one's heart. The square is marginalized and left on the edges of society.

"Well, that is my fate: and it is as natural for us Flatlanders to lock up a Square for preaching the Third Dimension, as it is for you Spacelanders to lock up a Cube for preaching the Fourth...when the Land of Three Dimensions seems almost as visionary as the Land of One or None; nay, when even this hard wall that bars me from my freedom, these very tablets on which I am writing, and all the substantial realities of Flatland itself, appear no better than the offspring of a diseased imagination, or the baseless fabric of a dream...Hence I am absolutely destitute of converts, and, for aught that I can see, the millennial Revelation has been made to me for nothing...Yet I exist in the hope that these memoirs, in some manner, I know not how, may find their way to the minds of humanity in Some Dimension, and may stir up a race of rebels who shall refuse to be confined to limited Dimensionality."

The Science of Spirituality

The above story shows why spiritual teachers are the connectors of the future. They glimpse a Reality beyond the three dimensional world that most humans perceive. They see something higher and deeper that connects all religions and peoples. Unity is the result of spiritual insight, and this insight is what transforms us from limited animals, perceiving that I am here and you are there, to something else, a new kind of being that perceives the world as interconnected, complete, united by something common to both you and me; something that makes us One. Haidt, being a Jewish atheist, interprets this oneness in evolutionary terms, which is very fine and accurate. Humans are not only selfish competitors; we've evolved altruism to care for our children. It's in our DNA to sacrifice for the group. In other words, we are more like bees than monkeys in many ways. We're designed to integrate and harmonize with the hive.

Moreover, there are neural correlates to this experience of oneness. And I quote Micheal Shermer.

"In a related study, researchers Andrew Newberg and Eugene D-Aquili found that when Buddhist monks meditate and Franciscan nuns pray, their brain scans indicate strikingly low activity in the posterior superior parietal lobe, a region of the brain the authors have dubbed the orientation association area, which orients the body in physical space. When the OAA is booted up and running smoothly, there is a sharp distinction between self and nonself. When OAA is in sleep mode, as in deep meditation and prayer—that division breaks down, leading to a blurring of the lines between reality and fantasy, between feeling in body and out of body...Perhaps this is what happens to monks who experience a sense of oneness with the universe, or with nuns who feel the presence of God."

Historically, religions have always functioned to orient an in-group against some enemy out-group. That is, spiritual leaders may or may not have been inspired by higher spiritual impulses, and even if they were, the conditions of their era may have forced them to use whatever inspiration they had to defeat enemy tribes in the name of survival. But survival is not the main purpose of religious pursuit. As William James and many others have observed, religion initially functioned to induce experiences of elevation and oneness in its followers. It functioned to elicit peak exp- eriences, and then, in the truly spiritual sects, to turn those peak experiences into more or less permanent states of being.

Maslow and positive psychologists today describe peak experiences as states essential to self-actualization. The qualities of this experience are described by Maslow in his book, Religion, Values, and Peak Experiences. Here are a few: (1) feelings of bliss, love, and gratitude. (2) altered perceptions of time and space. (3) perception of Reality as unified and connected. (4) disappearance of dualistic egotism as the self merges with something Else. (5) humility in the face of the ultimate mystery of existence.

All of these feelings combine to create goodness in the human person. The blurring of the distinction between self and other cannot help but create altruism and authentic moral and spiritual values. This blurring also leads to the creation of a detached witnessing self; a higher Self according to Hindu's. I often find myself outside of my body. Other times, I am inside my body. I can tell you from personal experience. The outside of the body Self is definitely more aware, peaceful, loving, and most importantly, conscious than the self I am when inside this body.

Peak experiences ennoble the individual soul. In today's world, they move us beyond kin altruism and reciprocal altruism, to a place of species altruism and bio-altruism; an orientation of good will towards all of God's creatures. The peak experience turns off the "I" meme and turns on the "We" meme. Elevation means love. Elevation means goodness. But elevation is only part of the story. Spirituality is about higher consciousness; a level of existence that most traditional religions have failed to share with their followers. As Maslow writes, religions have been taken over by men unwedded to something higher; to whom peak experiences have rarely if ever happened. Religions today are overrun by ritual, dog- ma, hierarchy, us vs. them memes, orthodoxy, and mind-made egotism. They are used to acquire money and power, and sometimes to kill and torture innocents. They have forgotten the true essence of the nature of God: love and oneness.

In today's world, we need to recapture that essential spirit of goodness, which is the foundation of all of the world's religions. Moreover, we have to create a spirituality enlightened by the progress made by mankind these past centuries. For many reasons, the majority of humanity is drenched in unconscious impulses and biases. Religion, once serving to elevate the human race, today keeps us in chains. That's why during every age small sects break away from the madness of traditional fundamentalist dogma. At their very foundation, most religions say the same thing: Goodness is love. Love is oneness. Oneness is elevation. Elevation is joy. Joy is goodness.

"Standing on the bare ground my head bathed by the blithe air uplifted into infinite space all mean egotism vanishes. I become a transparent eyeball; I am nothing; I see all; the currents of the Universal Being circulate through me; I am part or parcel of God". ~ Emerson

Love Meme

As mentioned, the I-It meme has one huge weakness. It degrades the connection between humans. Meanwhile, the I-You meme of goodness pumps up social networks with incredible energy and power. In his book, A New Earth, Eckhart Tolle gets to the very basis of why spiritual movements get off the ground. He calls spiritual teachers, Frequency Holders. They are connectors because they exude an energy that draws people towards them. Mark Matousek discusses the kind of energy spiritual teachers exude, using the example of the Dalai Lama.

"First was a "palpable goodness" that went far beyond some "warm and fuzzy aura". Next, an impression of selflessness—a lack of concern with status, fame, and ego. Third, [Paul] Ekman observed that this expansive, compassionate energy nurtured others. Finally, he was struck by the "amazing powers of attentiveness" displayed by individuals like the Dalai Lama, and the feeling one experienced of being "seen in the round", wholly acknowledge by someone with open eyes...Sociologists tell us that memes for virtue can elevate populations against the odds. As Colby and Damon note, "When the minority's behavior is perceived as both extreme and virtuous by the majority, sooner or later the majority will move in the direction of the admired minority."

Order is life. Chaos is death, for both the individual and human civilization. The saints and heroes of history serve as models for humanity. The smallest person can make the biggest difference. Not because Frodo is the only hobbit capable of taking the ring into the fires of Mt. Doom, but because the goodness of heroes such as Frodo serve to inspire millions, so that one hero doesn't have to do the job alone anymore. One day, there will no longer be a need for spiritual teachers; forget worldshaking titans such as Gandhi and Jesus. In the real world, there can be many Harry Potters and Samwise Gamgee's working to make the world a bit more lovely and brighter.

In his book, The Ways and Power of Love, Pitrim Sorokin gives another reason as to why the love meme is always going to proliferate over the hate meme. Yes, you have elevation. Yes, you have positive energy. Yes, you have flourishing memes traveling through flourishing social networks. But finally, you have the capacity for creative genius. Sorokin breaks down human personality into four basic parts. (1) The biologically unconscious aspect: the instinctive animal in man; all of the drives related to survival and growth. (2) The bioconscious: the autonomous ego, driven by personal ambitions and solipsistic desires. (3) The socioconscious: the part of our personality arising from social interactions with others; the roles, memes, and social scripts humans must play in the game of life. (4) The Supraconscious: the part of us that is more than us, allowing man to tap into energies and vibrations connected to some kind of higher Order, the Force, the Tao, the One, the Good.

Sorokin writes that the supraconscious inspires the highest achievements of human culture and creativity. There are two forms of love for Sorokin. Ego-centered love is narrow, weak, short, impure, and selfish to the core. But the love arising from our supraconscious is intense, broad, all encompassing, durable, and pure. It's a subtle high, so clean that you stop desiring things like sex and pot. "Like supreme creativity in the field of truth or beauty, supreme love can hardly be achieved without the direct participation of the supraconscious and without the ego transcending techniques of its awakening." The culmination of the supraconscious creates the personality of the "perfectly integrated creative genius" according to Sorokin. Following is an excerpt from my first book, The One, the Light, and the End of History.

Why Consciousness Determines Culture

Now let's consider the qualities of consciousness. The Harvard sociologist, Pitrim Sorokin, speaks of the nondualistic consciousness as a divine intuition that guides the destiny of humanity through the creative altruism of holy men. He calls it the supraconscious; a quality beyond the rational mind. It's a bright spark of creativity that inspires the greatest musicians, philosophers, and scientists of our time.

"Then my soul is on fire with inspiration, if however nothing occurs to distract my attention. The work grows. I keep expanding it, conceiving it more and more clearly until I have the entire composition in my head..." - Mozart

In his book, The Ways and Power of Love, Sorokin points to intuitive creativity as the force behind ethics. The greatest moral works come from sages under the influence of something beyond themselves. Jesus said I and the Father are one. The Buddha spoke of Nirvana and the extinction of the self. Both sages manufacture the energy of love through their creative altruism. Their lives are filled with this selfless and unitive force. So far, mankind has mastered the material realm through science, but we are woefully ignorant when it comes to the power of love. Sounds cheesy, right? But think about it. Love wins political struggles. Consider Gandhi and Martin Luther King. Its production is the highest aim of religion. In turn, love arises when the process of psychological reconciliation culminates inside the nondualistic being. Let's look at Abraham Maslow's psychological description of the nondualistic consciousness.

He writes "at the higher levels of human maturation, many dichotomies, polarities, and conflicts are fused, transcended, or resolved.

The person at the peak is godlike not only in the senses that I have touched upon already but in certain other ways as well, particularly in the complete, loving, uncondemning, compassionate and perhaps amused acceptance of the world and of the person."

Throughout history, sages speak to the utter simplicity of spiritual enlightenment and how it is within reach of all beings. What is the nature of this religious experience? The psychologist, William James, calls much of it a form of psychopathy, although a beneficial one to many who experience it. He says it's a particular temperament that takes to philosophy and metaphysics, and that individuals with certain psychological "quirks' ' are naturally predisposed to having joyous visions of what they interpret as God and Truth.

"but in reality the greatest of blessings come to us through madness, when it is sent as a gift of the gods.... the poetry of the sane man vanishes into nothingness before that of the inspired madmen." Socrates

"Since he separates himself from human interests, turns his attention toward the Divine, he is rebuked by the vulgar, who consider him mad, and do not know he is inspired." Plato

The nondualistic experience unifies the human psyche into seamless wholes. More specifically, it relates to heightened perceptions of reality as if the universe opens itself to the perceiver, and shows its underlying essence as being one and the same thing. Everything becomes perfectly itself, as it ought to be, with no perturbations in the still pond of conscious witnessing, and in which the world displays itself without limitations and borders.

"False imagination teaches that such things as light and shade, long and short, black and white are different and are to be discriminated; but they are not independent of each other....in essence things are not two but one." Lankavatara Sutra

"Jesus said to them: When you make the two one, and when you make the inner as the outer, and the outer as the inner and the above as the below, and when you make the male and the female into a single one, then you shall enter the Kingdom." Gospel of St. Thomas

"The Perfect Way is only difficult for those who pick and choose, Do not like, do not dislike, all will then be clear. Make a hairbreadth difference, and Heaven and Earth are set apart, If you want the truth to stand clear before you, never be for or against. The One is none other than the All, the All is none other than the One." Seng-Tsan

The nondualistic consciousness is the fount of love and religion. After an initial withdrawal into heavenly contemplation, it manifests itself in earthly endeavors through spiritual works and cultural transformation. Humans are naturally mimetic creatures. We copy what we see, and so the saint is a moral exemplar for all mankind. Seeing her goodness enlivens the goodness within us. The energy of love vibrates between human souls unseen, but felt deeply. There is proof of how a child given love grows into a healthy adult, while a child ignored grows fearful and violent. This is because every word and act impresses itself on consciousness. Energetic interactions never disappear entirely. Violence begets violence. Love creates love. If the world is to heal itself, then the energy of conscious love is the only tonic. This love emerges when humankind realizes the goodness that can only come from self-transcendence and the complete actualization of morality in consciousness. It emerges when beauty and goodness imbue themselves into every human soul on the planet by detaching spiritual consciousness (purusha) from the workings of animal nature (prakriti).

And so I imagine a future where all humans aspire to enlightenment through morality and meditation; when violence, rape, murder, war, and cruelty are things of the past; when our evening news no longer speaks of pain and suffering; when sad stories no longer pervade our airwaves. Can this future become reality? If the moral being takes the reins of power and guides humanity towards the Light, there is no telling how bright and beautiful our future will be.

"from this point of view we may admit the human charity which we find in all saints, and the great excess of it which we find in some saints, to be a genuinely creative social force. The saints are authors, auctores, increasers of goodness. The potentialities of development in the human soul are unfathomable...The saints, with their extravagance of human tenderness, are the great torchbearers of this belief, the tip of the wedge, the clearers of the darkness. Like the single drops which sparkle in the sun as they are flung far ahead of the advancing edge of a wave-crest or of a flood, they show the way and are forerunners." ~ William James

Flowful Deliberateness

Happiness is when what you think, what you say, and what you do are in harmony. ~ Gandhi

Despite the foray into new age hippie la-la land that I just made, the fact of the matter is that spirituality is not something that makes anyone different from anyone else. I know plenty of atheists that have more goodness and meaning in their pinky fingers than many so-called religious people. Aligning with your deeper and higher self does not require some specific set of beliefs. Indeed, as you dive into it, spirituality turns out to be something that bridges the gap between believers and non-believers. It's simply about conscious living, which anybody can do.

"So the most important thing to realize is this: Your life has an inner purpose and an outer purpose. Inner purpose concerns Being and is primary. Outer purpose concerns doing and is secondary. Your inner purpose is to awaken. It is as simple as that...Awakening is a shift in consciousness in which thinking and awareness separate. Opening yourself to the emerging consciousness and bringing this light into this world then becomes the primary purpose of your life....When doing becomes infused with the timeless quality of Being, that is success...The outer purpose of the universe is to create form and experience the interaction of forms — the play, the dream, the drama, or whatever you choose to call it. Its inner purpose is to awaken to its formless essence...Awakened doing is the alignment of your outer purpose – what you do – with your inner purpose – awakening and staying awake." ~ Eckhart Tolle

Finding your life purpose requires balancing contemplation with action. Pull inwards, find your deepest aspirations and dreams, and then act on them, constantly refining your plans as you go along. At the end of the day, we all have one purpose, which is to actualize the timeless Being inside of us, and imbue that awareness into material reality. I know this sounds super fancy, but it doesn't have to be. Making the best coffee you can for a customer is more significant if carried out in an awakened state than any politician governing the lives of millions. By these means, by aligning your conscious intention with awakened action, you fulfill God's plan, and enter what Mihalyi Csikczentmihalyi calls flow.

Remember, flow is the experience of timeless joy as action and awareness merge in the pursuit of meaningful, authentic, and challenging life goals. Aristotle believed that all things in the universe had a telos; an end towards which they aspire. For humans, our telos, the essence of the good life, is the coherence of arete (excellence) and eudaimonia (happiness) with our overarching life purpose. Human happiness is about realizing our highest potential, developing our strengths, and becoming the best of whatever we choose to be.

If this life purpose absorbs all of our energies and talents, if it results in uniting our individual drives with altruistic motives, if it merges the little droplet that is us with the universal currents of life, then life transforms us into one unified flow state, where each little action functions within a larger goal structure, and joy becomes a natural state of being because you just know that you're doing what you're meant to be doing, that you're going in the right direction.

In his brilliant book, Flow, Mihalyi, a psychology professor at Claremont, says the meaningful life, the ideal life, has three important qualities, allowing one to access a consistent state of flow that unites joy, awareness, and doing: (1) Directionality, which brings order to the contents of one's consciousness. (2) Intentionality, which is the gritty resolution, the umph of energy that forces order and structure upon one's life activities. (3) Harmony, the coherence of one's feelings, thoughts, and actions unified by a higher calling.

Ultimate Life Goals

Now, I don't want people to feel like their lives are worthless because they don't fit this ideal type of human being. More than anything, flow comes from loving what you do. And nothing is black and white. Most people have some degree of direction, intention, and harmony in their lives. It's just that some people go overboard and get crazy about finding meaning. Some people, for some crazy reason, aren't happy unless they're pursuing what Mihalyi calls ultimate life goals. These goals stretch beyond the individual's life. They ripple through the sands of time. They wrestle with issues of mortality, God, and the deepest aspirations of the human soul.

For example, Hannah Arendt speaks of the ultimates of western civilization. The Greeks aspired to immortality through glorious death by combat and heroic deeds. The Christians connected to eternal life through saintly acts. Hindus did it by chilling in caves. Atheists do it by considering the progress of history; how their actions whisper beyond the grave in the most inconceivable ways. And even the most "mundane" life goals, raising awesome children, accrue incredible significance if you look at it the right way. No one is less important than anyone else. Every human is essential to the progress and continuation of the human race.

Life Themes and Entropy

Once you realize how significant you are, then your ultimate goals begin to construct life themes; central ideals that every thought, behavior, and action tends to harmonize around. When your life energies are focused on a single point, "when a person's psychic energy coalesces into a life theme, then consciousness achieves harmony." But all life themes aren't good. They can be accepted or discovered, and discovered life themes often run roughshod over the conventions of the older generation. They push the frontier. They question the majority. They piss a lot of people off.

In what might be the best idea in his book, Mihalyi ties the thermodynamic concept of entropy to life, meaning, and morality. Entropy is the idea that closed systems tend towards disorder over time. Why? I have no idea. I think it has to do with the fact that usable energy is finite and the very process of using it transforms such energy into something dissipated and unusable. Think about our shrinking oil supplies, or think about how our sun's bountiful output keeps entropy on our little earth system from falling into disorder. Smart people say that entropy must grow until our universe either crunches or explodes many billions of years in the future.

In physical systems, entropy rises and there's nothing we can do about it. But in life systems, in the human soul, in what is the essence of spirituality, there exists an evolutionary urge towards some kind of self organization and order that transcends the chaos of the physical world. Mihalyi says that humans can fashion for themselves either entropic or negentropic life purposes.

"In a similar way, some people are able to bring the same sharp focus to their psychic energy throughout the entirety of their lives. The unrelated goals of the separate flow activities merge into an all encompassing set of challenges that gives purpose to everything a person does. There are very different ways to establish this directionality. Napoleon devoted his life, and in the process gladly led to the death hundreds of thousands of French soldiers, to the single-minded pursuit of power. Mother Teresa has invested all her energies to help the helpless, because her life has been given purpose by an unconditional love based on the belief in God, in a spiritual order beyond the reach of her senses."
~ Csikczentmihalyi

In the original Greek of the New Testament, the word sin does not mean "to commit an evil act". Instead, it means failure, being in error, or missing the mark. Sinners are not inherently evil people. They are simply lost souls; people with no purpose in life, drifting aimlessly in circles instead of finding their center. Other people, who one might call evil, are those who craft for themselves life purposes that increase the entropy of the world. As mentioned, evolution harmonizes parts into larger wholes. Cells work in your body just as individuals function inside the moral and legal framework of human civilization.

What is it that creates entropy, and what can pull us out of it? Simple. Sex, money, and power pull us into the darkness. Since they are finite resources, they create chaos as humans struggle to grab as much as they can. Power is relative. More for me usually means less for you; so is money. Meanwhile, the spiritual impulse, the higher Order in all of us, is the gift that keeps on giving. More light for me just creates more light for you. More for me, more for you. More for me, more for you. It's a process; a positive feedback loop of infinite proportions that results in the creation of social order, unity, and the future flourishing of human civilization. Perhaps, no story better represents my own hero's journey than Dante's Divine Comedy. Here's the basic tale.

"First of all, wandering in the dark forest, Dante realizes that three fierce beasts are stalking him...representing among other things, ambition, lust, and greed...the desire for power, sex, and money. To avoid being destroyed by them, Dante tries to escape by climbing a hill. But the beasts keep drawing nearer, and in desperation Dante calls for divine help. His prayer is answered by an apparition: the ghost of Virgil....Virgil tries to reassure Dante: The good news is that there is a way out of the dark forest. The bad news is that the way leads through hell. And through hell they slowly wend their way, witnessing as they go the sufferings of those who had never chosen a goal, and the even worse fate of those whose purpose in life had been to increase entropy—the so called 'sinners'." Csikszentmihalyi

Accepted Life Themes

It's the rare soul that crafts a self-discovered life theme. The majority of regular people model the lives of the great (or not so great) humans who have come before them. As mentioned throughout this book, humans are wired to learn through mirroring, suggestion, memes, and repetition. We have evolved to model the actions of others. Such modeling was once essential for survival. Today, it serves to create social epidemics of virtue vs. vice. Social networks fragment and cultural bubbles form as a natural result of our willingness to follow others.

In one group, you have warmongering Napoleon spreading memes of glory and conquest. In another, you have Mother Teresa giving her life to help the poor. Both individuals possess charisma and behaviors that we're designed to model. Napoleon primes our competitive drives. Mother Ter- esa does the same for our altruistic motives. Mihalyi writes, "The hero and the saint, to the extent that they dedicated the totality of their psychic energy to an all encompassing goal that prescribed a coherent pattern of behavior to follow until death, turned their lives into unified flow experiences. Other members of society order their own less exalted actions on these outstanding models, providing a less clear, but more or less adequate, meaning to their lives."

And here we encounter the most important purpose of the spiritual teacher. He or she serves to spread the meme of goodness, the meme of optimism, the meme of awesomeness. Let's look at that causal chain again from Angela Duckworth's book.

Interest —> A good purposeful role model —> A problem in the world that needs solving —> I can personally make a difference.

Purpose is one of the most powerful forms of motivation. Spirituality gives us purpose. Happiness is another big motivator. Spirituality gives us that too. And what about goodness, direction, community, and connection? Good spiritual teachers give humans everything they need for psychic order and harmony. Teachers are meaning creators; people of power and influence, who must take their responsibility seriously and push themselves to be the best models they can be.

Often, this sense of meaning comes from suffering, but it doesn't have to. Nevertheless, most men of God know how it feels to get kicked in the teeth, and so they work to make sure that it doesn't happen to others. They experience post-traumatic growth; a new sense of resilience found in the face of the personal failure and psychic chaos induced by the corrupt material world, by the entropy, surrounding them. Mihalyi writes, "To find purpose from suffering one must interpret it as a possible challenge. What transforms the consequences of a traumatic event into a challenge that gives meaning to life is the ability to draw order from disorder. Finally, a complex, negentropic life theme is rarely formulated as the response to just a personal problem. *Instead, the challenge becomes generalized to other people, or to mankind as a whole.*"

In short, altruism pulls us out of the darkness and into the light. The ideal human life is one that achieves coherence. A person is coherent when her instincts, coping mechanisms, life story, personality, consciousness, activities, and thoughts are all integrated into one self-supporting harmony. Moreover, this harmony is only achievable when the world around you allows it to happen. Either you bend to the world or the world bends to you. Greatness usually involves the second route, but it can also happen by the first, assuming the world around you is designed to create greatness within the individual soul instead of crushing it out of existence.

"Finding coherence across levels feels like enlightenment, and it is crucial for answering the question of purpose within life.....People are multilevel systems in another way: We are physical objects (bodies and brains) from which minds somehow emerge; and from our minds, somehow societies and cultures form. To understand ourselves fully we must study all three levels—physical, psychological, and sociocultural." ~ Jonathon Haidt

Ancient Virtues

For centuries, the cultivation of virtue and goodness remained the sole business of philosophers and holy men. Today, it's increasingly coming to light that, when it comes to actually walking the walk, psychology is more important than anything else for moral living. For example, brain scans have shown that if you want to be compassionate, you have to practice compassion. Neural connections form quickly and they disappear just as fast. Use it or lose it. Our brains are like muscles. If you want dense compassion neural networks and not-dense aggression networks, then you have to work at it. Neurogenesis and our brain's malleability is the source of hope for the future of mankind. We can change! We can change super fast if we put our minds to it.

The biggest problem is modern society. Everyone and everything becomes an It in our hurried world. The It is taking over. Instead of treating others as means to your own selfish ends, actually try to see the humanity in them. You can craft your brain into an organ that turns every human into a You. It's the I-You connection. I did this practice a while ago. By conscious focus, by controlling my mind, I started looking at people as a you. I attended to their words completely. And as if by magic, I started doing it naturally. Now (unless I'm being stupid, which happens), I attend most social interactions as a moment to exchange light and goodness, as a conscious process of connection. By being conscious, you bring out the consciousness in another.

As Haidt rightly points out, this process of morally sculpting the brain is something most ancient philosophers intuited. The Greeks, Indians, Chinese, Africans, Egyptians, and other cultures all knew that virtuous living depends on practice, habit, role models, and short insightful maxims. Meanwhile, modern philosophy worships the god of reason. No one cares about virtue anymore because the west has turned it into some dry exercise in proofs and logic. American culture is about food and money these days, not virtue and piety.

While modern thought set the basis for the construction of liberal democracy with its emphasis on individual rights, freedom, and the common welfare, modernity also set the groundwork for generations of suffering. Freedom isn't goodness. Freedom is chaos with the potential for goodness. When it comes down to it, goodness and even freedom arise from consistent self-discipline and habit. You can reason about good and evil all day, it won't make you a good human being. Ultimately, doing good arises from strengthening your neurons of goodness.

Many people are gritty about money and success, but very few consider the idea and its connection to virtue and conscious living. To illustrate, Haidt talks about his own habit of meat eating. He says that after reading Peter Singers book, Practical Ethics, which presents arguments against causing suffering to large brained social mammals, he felt guilt and hypocrisy every time he ordered a hamburger. In a fantastic line, he said he was morally opposed, but behaviorally complicit in the eating of meat. Why? Because I'm sure that he's been eating burgers since he was a child. Lifelong habits form neural bundles in the brain that are super difficult to override. The same thing happened in my case.

For both Haidt and myself, moral reasoning wasn't enough. We needed to recruit our deeper instincts, specifically the moral emotion of disgust. This impulse in the psyche once helped humans avoid poisonous foods. It's pivotal for survival and, after watching documentaries of what goes on in factory farms (cows being dismembered and stuff), disgust makes meat eating easier to drop. For Haidt, videos of suffering did what words could not. He stopped eating meat for a few weeks, and then begrudgingly took up the habit again.

Bottom line: Virtue is animal passion recruited in service of higher reason and awareness. This idea of passion in service of the good can be broadened to apply to every emotion, from sadness to elevation to anger. When it comes to altruism, perhaps the most powerful emotion is happiness.

And I quote Haidt: "The happiness-as-cause hypothesis received direct support when the psychologist Alice Isen went around Philadelphia leaving dimes in pay phones. The people who used those phones and found the dimes were then more likely to help a person who dropped a stack of papers (carefully timed to coincide with the phone caller's exit), compared with people who used phones that had empty coin-return slots. Isen has done more random acts of kindness than any other psychologist: She has distributed cookies, bags of candy, and packs of stationery; she has manipulated the outcome of video games (to let people win); and she has shown people happy pictures, always with the same finding: Happy people are kinder and more helpful than those in the control group."

In the book Flourish, Martin Seligman says that "we scientists have found that doing an act of kindness produces the single most reliable momentary increase in well-being of any exercise we have tested." Mix the focusing illusion, priming, happiness, random acts of kindness, the power of influence in social networks, the meme of goodness, grit, personal power and its positive connection to social power, elevation, associative coherence, intuition, neuroplasticity, modeling, positive feedback loops, crowds and power, both negative and positive emotions supporting each other in service of the Good, Oprah, meditation, tipping points, kale-kiwi plant protein smoothies, love, the power of artists inspired by the supraconscious, and a bunch of other stuff I've forgotten, and what you have is the future flourishing of human civilization, the overpowering flowering of human consciousness, the cultural explosion of the meme of goodness. You have the proliferation of awesomeness across the world. You have yourself...my friends...a love revolution.

Made in the USA
Columbia, SC
06 January 2025